Kingdom Partnerships for Synergy in Missions

William D. Taylor, Editor

William Carey Library
Pasadena, California, USA

Editor: William D. Taylor
Technical Editor: Susan Peterson
Cover Design: Jeff Northway

© 1994
World Evangelical Fellowship
Missions Commission

Published by:
William Carey Library
P.O. Box 40129
Pasadena, CA 91114
USA
Telephone: (818) 798-0819

ISBN 0-87808-249-2

Printed in the United States of America

Table of Contents

89997

PART THREE: INTERNATIONALIZING AGENCIES

APPENDICES

Preface

Dr. Michael Griffiths

I am excited about this book, because it speaks to a most significant missionary issue. Men and women of God have always been stirred up by Him to get things done: they are always dissatisfied with God's people as they are. Old Testament prophets were angrily disturbed, expressing God's own distress that His people were not the way He wanted them to be. The Apostles Paul, Peter, and John wrote because they were disenchanted with the way the church was, and they expressed God's own disappointment with His church. It is therefore thoroughly biblical for us also to be somewhat frustrated with the church!

Most missionary societies, including denominational ones, were started by individuals (Hudson Taylor, C. T. Studd) or small groups of stirrers (CMS, SIM, BEM, WUMS) frustrated with the inertia of the churches of their day, getting others to join them in fresh initiatives to preach Christ, save souls, and plant churches. Men and women have their eyes opened to unreached continents (so David Livingstone goes to Africa) or countries (so Hudson Taylor goes to China, the Melbourne Trio to Borneo in 1928, and others into Nepal in 1953). Most of us, like me, became conscious of the significant sodalities during student days. Urbana's circular corridor once paraded a choice of mission booths from Andes to the Zambesi. Currently the *Mission Handbook of US/Canada Protestant Ministries Overseas* lists around 800 agencies. In a country like Japan, there were some 140 foreign mission agencies listed from North America and Europe, and perhaps 190 indigenous Japanese denominations.

Today we have a different scenario, as more and more countries in Africa, Asia, and Latin America (I agree with Patrick Sookhdeo that we should stop talking about the First, Second, Third, and even Two Thirds World—it seems unlikely that God makes such distinctions between us!) have started sending missionaries. The Philippines boasted (is that the right word?) at least seven different Baptist Missions from North America. Korea seems to specialize in multiplying Presbyterian denominations. In these marvelous days when missionaries are no longer exclusively Caucasian "palefaces," it is a joy to meet colleagues who are Brazilian, Chinese, Indian, Japanese, Korean, and Filipino. But the prospect of each one of the denominations in each country developing its own separate missionary society, intent on reproducing its own denominational "tribalism" in several other countries opens up mind-boggling prospects of proliferation. If all these groups are to start and jealously preserve their own denominational and interdenominational churches, exporting their own church histories instead of allowing fellow Christians to develop their own, the resulting chaos will be multiplied *ad nauseam.* Division of organization, duplication of effort, dissipation of energies, and escalation of operating costs are increasing astronomically. Western individualism multiplies organizations as a carcinoma multiplies cells—and with not altogether dissimilar pathological effect upon the Christian body. In some ways, it mirrors the inefficient bureaucracies and corrupted distribution in secular agencies. Fortunately, there have always been those sensible souls who just got on with the simple task of saving souls, baptizing bodies, and planting churches.

This book shows that godly men (sadly there are no women contributors; the participants include three women and 90 men!) now sense the folly of following indefinitely multiplied individual exercise to its ultimate absurdity! (The New Testament gives us no models for this: the writers seem to have embraced this One Church, One Lord idea—extraordinary lack of appreciation of the value of competition and private enterprise!) And while I am sure there is much laughter in heaven every time a conference reports its findings, this one seems to offer us real hope of turning the tide of proliferation. It is significant that it is non-Western fellow Christians who think so much less individualistically and selfishly, who are pressing us all to act corporately and more responsibly, as Joshua Ogawa reminds us.

The idea is simple: we should never struggle to do something alone, that we can do better if we cooperate with others in "partnerships." While we all rejoice in our jubilees and centennials, we begin to realize that our human organizations and divisions, and even our origins, have no permanent validity or divine sanction to continue until the Lord's return. None of our existing mandates are written in stone. Many of our traditional societies show evidence of corporate Parkinson's and even organizational Alzheimer's. It will take some time to change all our mindsets—"partnerships" are already being classified into convenient subgroupings! But this book points us in the right direction. Differences among evangelicals are rarely doctrinal; they are usually little more than the accident of which group we belong to. Most of us could work equally well within other similar Bible-believing missions.

This is certainly the way ahead, but there are difficulties, which are well expressed in the book:

Firstly, that it is always easier to go it alone, whereas even a bilateral "partnership" takes time to arrange. Paul McKaughan, in a superbly sensitive and spiritual contribution, deeply conscious of God's sovereignty, wrestles with the time, energy, and expense of arranging for even two agencies to work together temporarily, let alone for any kind of multilateral partnership among several disparate groups. Theo Srinivasagam (IEM) speaks of the value of "networks" as the contemporary way of relating.

Secondly, there is a tension between flexibility and mobility of response on the one hand, and the need to see that there is agreement over goals and methods. Some want as much freedom as possible, while others know there is safety in having it all carefully spelled out beforehand. Frontiers' flexible approach whereby teams designated to particular areas work out their own diverse Memoranda of Working Agreement under the flexible umbrella of the mother organization may have a lot to teach us. The comment, "If you can do it by consensus, don't write a constitution," is a helpful one. If constitutions were so important, the Bible would have provided them. Over-organizing is a cultural kink of some Western societies!

Thirdly, there is the question of how far mobile, activist innovators of outreach are wise to tie themselves afresh to the inertia of the cumbersome, slow-moving, self-obsessed, denominational churches ("like a mighty tortoise" syndrome). Carey was first called a "miserable enthusiast" to propose the use of "means" by church leaders, and later the BMS withdrew their support from Serampore. The Church Missionary Society may be a respectable Anglican society today, but it began with a group of evangelical laymen and ministers, whom the church establishment would have labeled as "maverick." We cannot forget that most of our mission organizations came into existence in order to overcome church inertia, in spite of the denominational church rather than because of it. The absorption of the IMC into the WCC, and the "Babylonian Captivity of Mission" by the ecumenical churches, does not encourage us to trust church politicians obsessed with maintenance. Phill Butler raises the issue, and Theo Srinivasagam warns us of donor dictation and interference, like the stupidity of the home mission board that told its missionaries they must only use the King James Version in Japanese! Hudson Taylor had real difficulty maintaining that the field had final decision and not the London Council, who were horrified when he proposed to treat the new American Home Council as equal with themselves, rather than as a junior council. What was important is that both were equally subject to field sovereignty! It is those who work with national Christians and national churches who know what the issues are. You cannot make informed field decisions based on sanctified ignorance, whether it comes from London, Wheaton, or the Black Forest! Some recent North American legislation may be trying to put the clock back, if well-meaning but not so well-informed people want to dictate what happens in someone else's country. If you give a gift, then you should not dictate how the recipients must use it: treat your brothers as adults, not children. Yet as Ogawa reminds us, Asian Christians have a closer sense of identity with the sending church, and there is a greater responsibility to support on the part of the church. After all, the church is God's eternal plan, while parachurch groups are unsightly scaffolding, temporary expedients, means to an end and not an end in themselves. The most significant "partnerships" we have to work out, as Interserve's Tebbe and Thomson remind us, are those with the church—its bureaucracy, inertia, and lack of vision notwithstanding. When every believer throughout the whole church shares the missionary concern of the "miserable enthusiasts," the unfinished task will be completed.

Dr. Michael Griffiths
Professor of Missions Studies
Regent College
Vancouver, BC, Canada

The World Evangelical Fellowship Missions Commission

William D. Taylor

The WEF Missions Commission is a global network of national missions leaders, with many of its members fulfilling wider international roles.

Our Core Values

Our Essence: We serve as an international partnering/networking team—sharing ideas, information, and resources to empower the global missions movement.

Our Desired Goal: Worldwide, evangelical churches and in particular the missions arm of WEF regional and national member alliances will be equipped to carry out the Great Commission.

Our Vision: To bring closure to Christ's Great Commission through a dynamic, unified, global missions movement focused on effectively training and sending missionaries.

A Word of History

From the beginning of WEF's history, a global passion has motivated the founders. The emergence of active, indigenous missionary movements in Asia, Africa, Latin America, the South Pacific, the Caribbean, and the Middle East was the primary catalyst that led to the launching of the Missions Commission in 1977. Its fundamental intention was to address worldwide missions issues of common concern to its member bodies, with particular interest for the emerged and now maturing non-Western missionary movements.

The Missions Commission dates back to the early '70s and has had three Executive Secretaries: Dr. Chun Chae Ok (1974-1979), a pioneer Korean woman missionary to Pakistan; Dr. Theodore Williams (1979-1986), founder of the Indian Evangelical Mission, who also serves as the president of WEF and current chairman of the Missions Commission; and Dr. William Taylor (1986 to present), born in Costa Rica and a former career missionary to Guatemala.

The Commission is led by an Executive Committee of eight key leaders resident in the regions of the world they represent. The other members are generally executive officers of national or regional missions associations. The Commission consultants provide specialized expertise in the different areas needed for a global perspective. All told, there are some 47 active members from 24 nations.

The Commission Objectives

1. To promote dynamic cooperation among existing and emerging national and regional missions associations, by providing a platform for:

- Expressing relational networking.
- Exchanging information.
- Forging strategic alliances and partnerships.

2. To strengthen and aid in the development of missionary training programs and sending structures by:

- Facilitating the use of expert consultant resources.

- Publishing and distributing vital information and didactic materials.

- Facilitating the training of key Two Thirds World missions leaders.

3. To address critical concerns of international evangelical missions structures and their national and regional associations by:

- Creating investigative task forces with specific assignments and objectives.

- Administrating projects and programs to achieve defined ends.

The Commission Operational Units

The Missions Commission carries out its objectives through the following operational units:

Membership Network

The Missions Commission (MC) membership currently includes two primary categories: general members and consultants. This participatory body is kept informed of MC activities and represents it before constituencies in their own part of the world.

General Membership

The MC draws its membership primarily from WEF member associations. There are 31 persons currently serving from around the world. Executive officers of regional missions associations are automatically invited to be part of the MC. Other leaders from national mission agencies or associations may be invited to serve on the basis of their specific gifting and contribution to the work of the Commission. The normal term of service in WEF commissions is two years. The complete list of our membership is available upon request.

Consultants

In addition to the general membership, the MC Executive Committee may invite into membership persons who are specialists in missions by virtue of their experience and training, but who do not qualify for regular membership because they are not directly involved in a member association. The normal term of service is two years. A group of 10 expert consultants are currently serving with the MC in this capacity.

The Commission is led by the Executive Committee, comprised of one invited representative from each of the continental missions associations, whose nomination must be approved by the WEF International Council (IC). The Executive Committee with the approval of the WEF/IC appoints a commission Executive Secretary, supervises his work, approves staff appointments, reviews ministry goals and budget, and seeks the general welfare of the Commission. Other members of the Executive Committee are the Executive Secretary and invited staff members. The current Commission staff include Dr. William Taylor, Executive Secretary; Dr. Jonathan Lewis, Associate Secretary for Latin America and the Caribbean; and Dr. Raymond Windsor, Coordinator of the International Missionary Training Fellowship.

The International Missionary Training Program (IMTP)

This long-term project was initiated in 1989 following the Manila Consultation on Missionary Training, where 60 leaders from around the world discussed critical issues in missionary training. The IMTP focuses on effectively training and sending missionaries from all nations to all nations.

The IMTP includes the following components: the International Missionary Training Fellowship (IMTF), the International Missionary Training Associates Program (IMTA), and the International Missionary Trainers Scholarship Program (IMTS). The

IMTP and its related programs have represented the major thrust of the WEF/MC in recent years.

International Missionary Training Fellowship (IMTF)

Through ongoing research, this project seeks to identify missionary training programs and centers around the world and links them together through a directory published every three years. Dr. Raymond Windsor also produces the quarterly bulletin *Training for Cross-Cultural Ministries* from his New Zealand office. This publication focuses on training issues and gives news and information appropriate to the global missionary leadership as well as the training community.

International Missionary Training Associates Program (IMTA)

Strategic training resource persons are being steadily recruited, trained, and mobilized to help achieve the ends of the MC, particularly in missionary training programs. Currently 12 leaders form the IMTA team and actively serve in consultant roles. MC staff members are considered IMTAs.

International Missionary Trainers Scholarship Program (IMTS)

This program is designed to empower, through advanced missiological studies, key men and women who have clear potential contribution to missions and missionary training in their own national context.

WEF/MC Publications Program

Based on established needs, the WEF/MC contracts the production of key books and texts and helps publish and distribute these and other titles which meet critical missions needs in different parts of the world. When necessary, appropriate translation and adaptation are carried out. Dr. Jonathan Lewis is the Commission publications coordinator.

Task Forces

Task Force on Tentmaking

This task force relates to other evangelical world bodies in the discussion and promotion of tentmaking missionaries. Dr. Jonathan Lewis has edited a unique course in workbook form, *Working Your Way to the Nations: A Guide to Effective Tentmaking*. The book utilizes 12 authors from 10 different countries and is designed for adaptation and publication in six other languages.

Task Force on Muslim Ministries

This task force has developed a global list of key leaders in Muslim ministries, assesses current training for this specialized ministry, and convenes consultations as needed.

Task Force on Non-Western Missionary Families

This task force is examining the needs of non-Western missionary families, with specific interest in counseling for the entire family and a focus on their missionary children.

If the WEF Missions can be of service to you, please do not hesitate to contact us at one of our international offices:

> William D. Taylor, Executive Secretary
> WEF Missions Commission
> 4807 Palisade Drive
> Austin, TX 78731, USA
> TEL: 512 467 8431
> FAX: 512 467 2849

> World Evangelical Fellowship
> International Headquarters
> 141 Middle Road, #05-05
> GSM Building
> SINGAPORE 0718
> TEL: 65 339 7900
> FAX: 65 338 3756

World Evangelical Fellowship
North American Offices
P.O. Box WEF
Wheaton, IL 60189, USA
TEL: 708 668 0440
FAX: 708 669 0498

1

Introduction:
Setting the Partnership Stage

William D. Taylor

"**W**hen are we going to sign the partnership agreements, Bill?" This pointed question was posed to me by a dear and godly Asian colleague in the course of the second day of our June, 1992, Manila conference, "Towards Interdependent Partnerships." It caught me by surprise, because even as coordinator of the conference, I frankly had not thought that actual commitments would be discussed, shaped, and agreed upon for implementation so soon. It seemed impossible!

The Background of the Consultation

Under the leadership of the WEF Missions Commission, that intense week brought together 95 missions leaders from 35 nations representing every continent and region of the world. They also represented the cream of international cross-cultural leadership who provide sensitive guidance to indigenous, national movements, as well as regional or international groups. They came from tiny nations such as the Solomon Islands to giants such as Brazil; from nations struggling with deep social injustice and poverty such as South Africa to economic powerhouses like Japan; they came from nations with over 200 years of missions like the UK to those with a young and emerging movement such as Guatemala; they came from sensitive countries of the Middle East to open nations like the Philippines; they came from the so-called "West" to the so-called "non-Western" nations. It was a godly rainbow coalition!

We had come not necessarily to sign agreements on the spot but to discuss the sensitive issues related to developing partnerships. We had come to examine the biblical standards, to evaluate the spectrum of models presented in plenary sessions, to discover how organizational structures and leadership styles affect partnerships. From that foundation we would then be equipped to initiate the kind of dialogue that could lead to partnership ministries.

I was greatly surprised to discover that the ministries represented at the consultation were already involved in more than 1,000 distinct partnerships. That meant the high privilege of listening to and interacting with men and women who were not partnership novices or simple theoreticians. We were engaging with cross-cultural servants who came to the table with a long history and personal experience in tangible ministry cooperative agreements.

Before the mid-point of the consultation, obvious tensions emerged in some of the participants. This was an initial surprise to me as a leader, and it was Phill Butler who analyzed the dynamics of the meeting with his vast experience in consultations. We had all come with very distinct and different expectations. Some were already impatient with the process, while others felt that too many plenary speakers were neutralizing the role and value of the small group dialogue. Some present had attended countless numbers of international meetings ("conference groupies!"), while others were attending their first-ever international forum. Phill was given program time early the next morning to share the "life cycle" of these consultations. It was an open acknowledgment of the tensions and a desire on the part of the leaders to flex with the needs and modify the program. The proper adjustments were then made in the schedule.

Alex Araujo later shared with me some of his insights in light of the participant differences. His grid proved helpful and even humorous.

Constituency	Expectations	Consultation Format	Corresponding Emotion
Beginner	To learn, to see what's available	A trade fair	"Wow!"
Operators	How to, strategy, tools, techniques	A workshop, a laboratory	"Let's get on with it!"
Grievants	To air grievances, redress wrongs, unload	Problem- solving, group therapy	"I've gotta say this!" or, "He hit me, Mommy!"
Devout	Fellowship	A spiritual retreat, worship, relationships, the body	"Praise the Lord for His mercy!"

It was impossible to meet everyone's expectations, but in very tangible ways the Holy Spirit made Himself known to us. The daily program had started with worship followed by the exposition of the Scripture by Theodore Williams, and then a time of prayer. From then until lunch we received the various issue papers with their plenary responses and discussion. The afternoons were primarily dedicated to small group dialogue based on the morning theme plus time for networking and relationship-building. The evening plenary sessions gave occasion to present partnership models and to conclude the day with another season of worship and prayer.

A Brief Definition of Partnership

There is a cluster of terms which are related to partnerships. Some of these include cooperation, teamwork, networking, joint ventures, and strategic alliances. We gave the consultation participants a list of these concepts with working definitions, which are included in one of the appendices of this book.

The simplest definition of partnership is "using mutual gifts to accomplish tasks." But Luis Bush offers a more complete, practical and helpful definition of partnership. It is "an association of two or more autonomous bodies who have formed a trusting relationship, and fulfill agreed-upon expectations by sharing complementary strengths and resources, to reach their mutual goal."*

This expression lays out the essential components of partnership. While we might analyze the definition and discuss its application for the consultation, I prefer to let it stand as the foundational affirmation of what we are attempting to communicate.

Impressions of the Consultation

As the week developed, a number of matters came into clear focus. First, there was a sense that the Spirit Himself had convened us; and the extended times of worship and prayer invited His presence. Secondly, the presentation and discussion of major partnership issues were valuable and the spectrum of working partnership models important. Thirdly, perhaps facilitated in light of the cultural diversity represented by the participants, the core values that characterize significant partnerships (particularly expressing the desires of the non-Western colleagues) emerged. Essentially they focused on relationships that grow after extended time for developing trust and mutual understanding. The terms "personal relationship," "time," and "trust" came up repeatedly. Some Western groups are perceived as tending to focus on functional, tangible, measurable, task-oriented, cooperative agreements. These come across as management programs, lacking the personal dimension of gracious mutuality in the body of Christ.

---

* Bush, L., & Lutz, L. (1990). *Partnering in ministry: The direction of world evangelism* (p. 46). Downers Grove, IL: InterVarsity Press.

Fourth, we realized our program was unexpectedly silent on some topics. One example was the issue of accountability; it simply had not been considered appropriately. Fortunately, Alex Araujo had worked the subject in depth and we were able to flex the program to insert him. But we were woefully weak on the topic of the local church in partnership, a fact addressed in a plenary session by Dan Davis, one of the pastors present. And while we dealt with the internationalization of mission agencies, some felt that our emphasis tended to focus too much on the positives. It was good to have Joshua Ogawa deal with that sensitive issue in his gracious but frank paper.

We simply did not engage the topic of the internationalization of mission and its relationship to partnerships. And this omission sparked off quite heated discussions in the halls. There is a clear differentiation between staff internationalization of mission agencies and the internationalization of the missionary movement. The latter speaks of "...the transcending of national boundaries, not only in reaching the goal of our mandate, but in the processes of planning, organizing and implementing the mandate."* Samuel Escobar has a penetrating article in which he also defines and grapples with some of the issues related to the internationalization of mission.**

Fifth, one clear problem emerged—that of language. The consultation language was English—for better or for worse, the global missions *lingua franca*. For many, therefore, it was easy to use key terms that had clear meaning and significance, such as: partnership, accountability, synergy, networking, task-oriented partnerships, strategic alliances, measurable outcomes. Having spoken Spanish all my life, I already realized that terms clear to the English language simply did not translate easily, even when the speaker is seeking some kind of dynamic equivalent. "Accountability" in Spanish is related

---

* Hann, P. (1983). Breaking the power habit: Imperatives for multi-national mission. *Evangelical Missions Quarterly, 19*(3), 180.

** Escobar, S. (1992). The elements of style in crafting new international mission leaders. *Evangelical Missions Quarterly, 28*(1), 6-15.

more to accounting and finances; so an expanded phrase has to be used, and even then it leaves much to be desired. In some of the African countries, "partnership" still has heavy and negative colonial overtones. It thus became a challenge to use the words and then overlay them with multiple definitions and near synonyms. It was not an easy task.

An Overview of the Book

Essentially we have taken the basic papers given in Manila, edited them, and reproduced them. Some chapters were written specifically to fill in a gap not dealt with in Manila.

The title was selected with clear purpose. We are discussing partnerships for the kingdom of the living God. We are promoting cooperative ventures, strategic alliances, mutually shared projects, and the sharing of material and human resources for the Cause of Christ. We are urging the church/missions community to go far beyond simple sharing and fellowship, moving further than networking. We are stressing the need for leaders and ministries to combine their forces for the common good. The term "synergy" is a fascinating one and rather new for many of us. The dictionary defines it as "combined action, the cooperative action of two or more stimuli, muscles, nerves, or the like." A synergistic effect in physiology speaks of a body organ that cooperates with others to produce or enhance an effect. One observer states that "synergism occurs when the output is greater than the sum of the inputs. For example, using an illustration from nature, one draft horse can pull four tons. If you harnessed two draft horses together, they can pull twenty-two tons." Synergy comes from partnerships; and we want to see kingdom partnerships for world missions.

Part One deals with partnership foundations. Phill Butler addresses the critical structural issues of partnership. Both an Indian leader, Theodore Srinivasagam, and an Englishman, Stanley Davies, respond with their own reflections to Phill's paper.

Part Two looks at three sensitive topics that profoundly affect partnerships. Patrick Sookhdeo with his characteristic insight nails down some of the critical cultural dimensions, and three different leaders from three different cultures (Paul McKaughan from the USA, Maikudi Kure from Nigeria, and Federico Bertuzzi from Argentina) respond to Patrick. Jun Vencer tackles the issue of control, particularly in church/mission relationships. Finally, Alexandre Araujo faces the sensitive matter of accountability, not as control but as a two-way trust relationship.

Part Three focuses on the internationalization of mission agencies as a viable model of partnership. Both Jim Tebbe and Ron Weir speak from the perspective of the West, but it is Japanese Joshua Ogawa who pointedly analyzes the advantages and disadvantages of Asians serving under leadership from a dominant global culture.

Part Four introduces us to a spectrum of seven partnership models. We have attempted to present models from Asia, North America, Africa, and Latin America. Unfortunately, most of the models were success stories, and we should have had some candid admission of frustration and failures.

And briefly, I draw conclusions and peer to the future of partnerships in missions.

The appendices bear mention as a fascinating variety of matters worth evaluating: from definitions of key terms (note in particular Tokunboh Adeyemo's taxonomy of partnerships); to actual written guidelines for partnership agreements; to an appeal from India for the rest of the world to be careful in their hasty partnerships within India; to a list of the consultation participants; and finally, a brief bibliography of helpful resources.

A Final Word

Perhaps the greatest fear in producing a book like this one is that, assuming it is even purchased, it simply goes on the shelf along with the other ones that perhaps someday might be perused. If such is the case, then the cause of kingdom partnerships is not advanced. May the Spirit somehow anoint these pages, chapters, thoughts, and directions in ways that accelerate the advance of the kingdom of Christ.

"Bill, can I share with you some good news about this week?" It was my same dear Asian colleague, speaking on the last day of the consultation. "I have been discussing with the leadership of another mission in our country, and we have come to conclusions about establishing a new partnership to take the gospel to an unreached people numbering some 300,000. We will combine our differing strengths: prayer, spiritual warfare, pioneer evangelism, linguistics and Bible translation, church planting, and teaching. Is this not good news, brother?" I could hardly contain myself! The leaders of these two national Asian mission agencies had traveled thousands of miles to Manila where they entered into the new partnership.

That kind of news makes a consultation viable and valuable!

William D. Taylor is the Director of the Missions Commission of World Evangelical Fellowship. A son of missionaries, born in Costa Rica, he served with his wife as a career missionary at the Central American Theological Seminary in Guatemala, Central America, as well as in church planting. He was a missions professor at Trinity Evangelical Divinity School and has taught in other seminaries in the USA, UK, and the Two Thirds World.

Part One: Foundations of Partnership

2

Kingdom Partnerships in the '90s: Is There a New Way Forward?

Phillip Butler

There seems to be consensus that effective partnerships are vital for the church. Few would argue against partnerships, at least in principle, particularly as we think about missions and the unfinished task of world evangelization.

There is the biblical motivation of blessing, power, and credibility that suggests such practical expressions of unity are essential. The rapidly changing world order of the '80s and '90s with strategic alliances in the international business world, even between fierce competitors, now assumes that such alliances are an integral part of any successful strategy. Rapidly shifting resources, particularly in missionary personnel, from Western to non-Western countries demand new ways of working together. In addition, funding and praying constituencies, with increasing information about our field operations, are asking critical questions about duplication of effort and lack of coordination.

In short, we can no longer ask, "Should we find ways of working together?" The only real issue, it seems, is how we can work together most effectively—learning from the past and looking to the future.

In the course of this paper, I will return to the question of motivation and world trends regarding partnership. But my real concern is dealing with the practical, working issues of partnership. We'll look at the past to see what we can learn and to the future to suggest some of the opportunities and issues we will face as we respond to Christ's call to go "to all people everywhere and make them my disciples...."

As most of you know, Bill Taylor, Executive Director of the WEF Missions Commission, wisely agreed to ask for feedback and input into the agenda for the Commission's meetings in Manila in June, 1992. Through a questionnaire, participants were asked to share something about their experiences in partnerships in the past—both the good and the bad; where partnerships have been helpful and where there were problems.

> *Achmed, a man in a "closed" country, came to Christ after having had contact with five different ministries. Radio, literature, Bible correspondence courses, visiting national evangelists, and local "tentmakers" all had a part. The key was their knowledge of each other and the conscious coordination of their efforts as Achmed was passed from one ministry to another in an active, working partnership.*

Participants' Assessment of Partnerships

Let me first summarize some of the trends that emerged as the feedback questionnaires were analyzed.

First, every respondent indicated that they had been or were now involved in some type of partnership. So, on the surface at least, it appears we were agreed that the topic is relevant!

Second, here are the issues that were most frequently cited as causing the most problems in partnership relationships—in order:

1. Cultural differences.
2. Lack of effective communications.
3. Financial issues.

4. Personality conflicts.

5. Lack of clear objectives.

Any surprises? One was the almost complete lack of significant comment about theological issues as a recurring problem in partnerships. One wonders what this might mean or say to us? Is it possible that much of what has been said in the past about theological differences keeping us from practical cooperation has really been a handy excuse—a way to avoid the hard work about real partnership issues—issues such as communications, objectives, money, and personalities?

But there was not agreement on everything. For example, in the responses there were 10 issues listed as problem areas in partnership experiences. One of the rather striking things that came through was that, in seven of these, the perceptions regarding the problems were markedly different between Western and non-Western leaders. Here are the issues where Western and non-Western leaders differed most in their perception of the problems:

1. Lack of clear objectives (non-Western leaders cited a much higher level of dissatisfaction on this issue than did their Western counterparts).

2. Lack of understanding/sensitivity to the political and economic problems in the region.

3. Problems with the agreements between the partner ministries.

4. Personality conflicts.

5. Lack of effective communications.

In general, there was a 32 percent higher sense of *dissatisfaction* regarding partnership experiences among non-Western leaders. And, on the issues where they differed with the Western leader counterparts on the importance of the problems, their dissatisfaction was, on average, *82 percent higher* than that of their Western counterparts!

Not surprisingly, the most consistent difference of opinion about problems dealt with communications issues: things like lack of clarity in agreements; lack of defined objectives; lack of effective, ongoing communications between the partner agencies; and so forth. Consistently, feedback suggests that the non-Western leaders have not only been less satisfied with previous partnership agreements, they have also been more aware of the problems than their Western counterparts have been.

The feedback also documented some of the trends in partnership that are emerging as we leave the '70s and '80s and move well into the '90s. For instance, the changing role of Western churches in the non-Western world. The non-Western mission leaders reported a high number of direct linkages or partnerships between Two Thirds World mission agencies and churches in the West. The same non-Western leaders reported a significant number of direct church/church partnerships, that is, Western and non-Western churches linking hands for ministry. In contrast, almost none of the Western respondents to the study (mostly mission agency executives) indicated any direct role for the Western churches in partnerships with counterpart mission agencies in the Two Thirds World!

Might this be due to fear on the part of the Western agencies that by actively bringing Western churches into a *direct role* in partnership, they, the agency, are somehow losing control?

Later in this paper we will return to some of these issues as we look into the '90s.

> One *effective partnership said, "We knew there were going to be problems. You can't attempt what we're attempting with people from such different backgrounds and not have small or large problems arise." The partnership credited the key to their success, among other things, with setting up a process in the beginning to deal with differences that would arise—in understanding of objectives, personnel issues, financial, administrative, or "cultural" differences. The "monitoring group" met regularly to identify and resolve problems before they ever got too big.*

Different Partnerships, Different Tasks

While there have been problems and differences about how successful partnerships have been, what about the *types* of partnerships that have been tried?

It is clear that the dominant form of partnership has been bilateral. For example, one entity links up with another, be it church/church, church/mission, mission/mission, east/west, or north/south partnerships. There have been some multi-agency partnerships where three or four missions have joined hands for a specific project, either a one-time project or a specific outreach that was well-defined and limited in its objectives. And there have been some networks and fellowships that have been called partnerships, such as mission agencies meeting to share information and in some cases developing plans and sharing resources for ministry in a nation, region, or people group.

Reviewing all these types of partnerships, it appears there has been and continues to be a valuable role for them all—as long as they are carefully conceived and sensitively conducted.

Since 1986, another form of partnership has begun to emerge called the "vertically integrated" form of partnership: various ministries coming together specifically to pray, plan, and work together over the long term for evangelism and the building of a church among a major unreached people group. These partnerships are called "vertically integrated" because they represent a conscious effort to get all the key elements needed to reach a particular people group together—from Scripture translation to mass media, development work to personal witness—each playing its own unique role but all linked in a conscious commitment to a common objective.

To understand this type of partnership more fully, we might consider what a "horizontally integrated" network might look like. Consider Scripture translation. There is a very complex, large, worldwide community of similarly minded specialists linked together for a single purpose: the effective translation of Scripture. There are educators, administrators, training programs, journals, international conferences, etc., horizon-

tally linked worldwide for the single task of Scripture translation. However, as critical as it is to building the church,
translation does not represent a complete evangelization strategy for a city, people, or language group.

When it comes to a specific language group, Scripture
translation must be "vertically integrated" with other forms of
witness. Ministries such as literature, broadcasting, personal
witness and discipleship, relief and development, medical
work, etc., all play unique roles and make unique contributions to establishing a healthy, nationally led church.

Ministries focused on their own specialty frequently are
consumed with the "means" rather than with the ultimate
"end," the building of the church. This is particularly true with
the increased proliferation and specialization of mission agencies. Often this focus on the means rather than the end results
in isolation, lack of communication, and fragmentation in
results—all qualities that are the antithesis of what partnership is all about. By participating in one of these "vertically
integrated" partnerships, ministries can play their specialized
role, yet be part of a coordinated effort focused on a common
objective.

There are at least 10 of these "vertically integrated" partnerships already operating among as many language groups.
Frequently these "vertically integrated" partnerships have
"horizontally integrated" networks, working groups, or specialized sub-partnerships within them. For instance, in one such
"vertically integrated" partnership, four or five broadcasting
agencies have their own working group or "horizontally integrated" specialized network. Linked together with other ministry partners, the broadcast group forms a vital part of an overall
strategy with other mission agencies reaching that people
group.

Interestingly, while there are over 200 different mission
agencies involved in these various "vertically integrated" partnerships, nearly one-third of them are non-Western. And less
than 40 percent are North American. Another dozen or so of
these "vertically integrated" partnerships are in various stages
of development in different language or people groups.

One "vertically integrated" partnership of over 30 min-
istries working in a highly resistant Islamic area has
formed cooperative media production units, joint technical
facilities, interagency Scripture and literature distribution
systems, a coordinated follow-up effort, and is now work-
ing on new joint leadership training programs. Their joint
efforts have saved several hundred thousand dollars and
have brought an equal amount of new money into the
region for expanded ministry. And, it is all done by con-
sensus—with no constitution!

Motivation for Partnerships: The Scripture

As we look ahead to the '90s, what is the real motivation for
partnership? If, while acknowledging the real and potential
problems, there is consensus that partnerships are important—*why* are they important?

First, of course, is the biblical foundation. God Himself
dwells in community—outside of time, in eternity. Wide-rang-
ing sections of Genesis, Job, Daniel, and Ephesians, not to
mention other Scripture portions, speak of God as dwelling in
a community of personalities or beings. It is not surprising,
then, that creating in kind, God made man to dwell in *relationship*, first with Himself and then with others. It was this
relationship that was so deeply damaged in Eden. The silence
and fear that haunted the Garden that day were only a foretaste
of the alienation man would face generation after generation
into the future.

It is about the restoration of this damaged relationship that
Jesus spoke in Luke 10 when questioned about salvation by
the young lawyer. The Apostle Paul carries the theme further
when he talks of our role as "agents of reconciliation" in
2 Corinthians 5.

Further, we see from Genesis to Revelation that witness is
always to be at two levels: individual *and community*. While
there is a clear role for individual witness outlined in Scripture,
both the Old and New Testament suggest that, in the end,

community witness is far more powerful. As Jesus states in John 17:20-23, it is the restored relationships and resulting functional community that is the basis for the credibility of our witness.

Tragically in the West, with the rise of individualism since the Enlightenment and the resulting loss of community, functional Christian practice (if not theology) has been heavily influenced. The result has been not only a loss of the joy, blessing, and accountability that come with such community, but also a distortion of our missions strategy and practice. Particularly Western mission agencies have been heavily influenced by this individualistic approach—frequently in how they are organized and in how they perceive their "call" or "vision." Frequently a call to a certain place or vision for a particular type of ministry is not confirmed through consultation with others, in a community of believers committed to a common objective. Rather, it is highly individualistic leadership that makes such decisions unilaterally.

And, ultimately, individualism has a powerful effect on the actual form of witness among unreached audiences and on how "success" is measured as the audience responds.

In traditional cultures, the deepest values are tied up in community, family structures, and other relational obligations. Whether it is Islam, Hinduism, or Buddhism, family, caste, or community exert powerful influences on individuals— their hopes, expectations, and ability to make decisions.

As we bring the Good News of the Lord Jesus, until we can offer an alternative community equal to or better than the one we are asking the individual to leave, what do we really have to offer? Jesus' words of John 17 ring in our ears as we wonder why the credibility, power, and apparent "breakthroughs" are lacking in so many of these so-called "resistant" cultures.

Beyond these issues, Scriptures like Psalm 133 point to the power of God's Spirit being released when believers dwell in unity. Do we want God's Spirit to empower our efforts? We must find ways to work with brothers and sisters in Christ in practical unity. The most resistant, challenging, unreached people groups remind us that our goal is not to be won with "guns and money." This cosmic struggle will only be won through the energizing release of the Holy Spirit's power.

These biblical themes suggest that partnerships which allow us to demonstrate at least functional community—to be aware of, pray for, speak well of, and support each other—are not an option: they are *absolutely critical.*

> *A recent convert in a "closed" country traveled to a Western country where he reported, "I was asked, 'What kind of church do you belong to?' I found this confusing and discouraging since I was a Christian and thought that was all I had to be."*

Motivation for Partnerships: World Conditions

One cannot pick up an international business publication without reading articles or advertising about strategic alliances between major corporations, many times between those who have been the most intense competitors.

All of the following provide motivation for cooperation in the world of the multinational corporation:

- Increased competition.
- A "global market" rather than national markets.
- A communications/information-based environment in which ideas and information travel at electronic speed.
- Widely distributed economic and technical resources.
- New demands for efficiency and profitability.
- The high risk of new ventures.
- The cost of new project development.

Like it or not, the international corporate cultures are leading the way in this post-modern world to structures that are "flatter," less hierarchical, and much more interactive and participative. The business world has come to see that there must be a conscious effort to build on internal strengths and

to "outsource" or go outside of themselves for all other requirements, by joining hands with other companies. The old days
of doing it all yourself or going it alone are over. It is the ability
to conceive, formulate, and sustain value-added strategic alliances that is the wave of the future.

On the religious side, there are growing alliances between
political and religious blocs with formidable power and specific
opposition to the gospel. These are increasingly frequent—particularly in Islam and militant Hinduism. Population studies
reveal that the fastest growing areas align remarkably with
those power blocs that are most resistant to Christ. Donors are
increasingly informed and aware of our work in the field. As a
result, they are more frequently asking questions about duplication of effort and about how our individual ministries fit into
the overall picture.

Finally, there is the reality that non-Western personnel will
soon be the majority of the Protestant missionary force and
already are a *major* factor in missions strategies.

If biblical imperatives were not enough, certainly these
world conditions provide a motivation for us to pray, plan, and
work together in partnership.

> *"The church is unaware of the momentous nature of
> this moment in history, of the radical changes that are
> taking place in the fundamental structures and fabric of
> the world order. They have not begun to see, much less
> understand the implications for our strategies, available
> resources, and operating policies."*
>
> — *Missions professor, 1992*

Motivation for Partnerships:
Mission Effectiveness

Experience over the last six to seven years shows that no
matter how lofty our motivations may be in the beginning,
ultimately a mission or church leader must or will ask himself,
"How does this alliance or partnership help my group realize
our ministry's vision more fully?" In short, mission agencies

must be able to identify specific, tangible benefits from the partnership that would not be realized if they were working strictly on their own.

What might some of those benefits be? Here is a short list of ways in which we have seen mission agencies benefit from being in an active partnership. The list is by no means comprehensive. And, for some agencies, other issues not on the list may be far more important.

1. Mission or church leadership may see that they have certain strengths but that opportunities before them call for additional resources—financial, technical, or human. To be able to contribute in an area where we have strengths while joining hands with other ministries for the missing elements simply makes sense. It also happens to be a basic scriptural principle (Rom. 12, 1 Cor. 12, Eph. 4, etc.)!

2. Partnerships allow a mission or church to enter new areas at reduced risk—joining hands with other ministries in research, legal, logistical, or training needs. Ministries have even recruited personnel jointly for a new region, raised funds together, and found ways to combine other Kingdom resources so that, together, they could do a job at much lower cost or "risk" than any could have done alone.

3. Working partnerships enhance the likelihood of attracting new operational resources (people, money, etc.) that might never have been available working individually. Donors, for instance, are increasingly attracted to joint enterprises that reduce duplication and increase the likelihood of effective ministry.

4. By being involved in partnership, mission agencies can often see their comparatively modest investment transformed into a major commitment of Kingdom resources. This "leveraging" of our resources, seeing a high rate of return on a comparatively modest but wisely made investment, is the type of risk-taking that Jesus speaks of in Matthew 25:14-30.

5. Evangelism partnerships that are strategic in nature and long-term in commitment allow their participants to understand where they "fit in," and to see the role God is giving

them with much greater clarity. This frequently is a particular blessing to missionary personnel, who then realize they are not alone in the struggle. For missionary leadership, it is good to be able to report that they have carefully, prayerfully analyzed the needs of the people group or region and are, along with others, responding in Christ's name with a specific, appropriate evangelism strategy.

One partnership helped several missions draft and circulate a joint funding proposal to new and existing donors—resulting in increased project income. Another formed a joint language training center so that all incoming personnel could benefit—something none could have afforded to do alone. Another brought five radio agencies together for a new, joint evangelistic outreach that is producing significant response from Muslim listeners in the region. And still another partnership was able to link the resources of a group of Western churches with priority needs in the region—identified, agreed on, and coordinated through the entire partnership.

Partnership Problems: Practical Steps

Let's return now to the key partnership problems which both non-Western and Western leaders have cited. My comments here are based in part on the input through the questionnaires mentioned at the beginning of this paper. They also draw on interviews and discussions with mission and church leaders, plus our field experience in partnership development with ministries from over 40 countries in the last seven years.

Cultural Differences

Under this broad heading, many problem areas are deftly hidden: policies, expectations, money, personalities, theology, accountability, and a host of others.

We may acknowledge that we are involved in cross-cultural ministry. However, it is remarkable how frequently Christian leadership can and do gloss over the deep differences in worldviews, assumptions, social dynamics, decision-making processes, and expectations between cultures. And, in so doing, we set ourselves up for, at best, great difficulty; at worst, failure.

What are some of the things that we can do to reduce problems rising out of our cultural differences?

First, we must start by acknowledging that these differences probably do exist and may have (potentially) serious impact on the partnership or project.

Second, we must be prepared to take our colleagues in partnership seriously—acknowledging that what they believe and say born out of their experience are likely to be just as valid as our own position. This means we must approach each other with respect and a genuine *desire*, not just a *willingness* to listen. As part of this, we must acknowledge that while Scripture judges all cultures, our perception of Scripture is often very ethnocentric or culturally based. We do not necessarily have the "right" answer for all circumstances, particularly in matters of operational policy that might affect working partnerships. Assuming that we can extend our own cultural norms (often themselves not truly Christian) to another culture frequently spells disaster.

Third, we must be prepared to take the time to talk through, in considerable detail, our *mutual* understanding of key elements in any partnership—concepts, specific words used, standards, etc. Here are some issues that are frequently troublesome and deserve detailed time and reflection:

• What are our objectives in the partnership: short, medium, and long-term? How do we define "success" in meeting these objectives? For instance, are the objectives such that they can be evaluated statistically? Are the objectives bound up in more difficult-to-evaluate elements, such as behavior, relationships, or attitude change? If so, are we looking for this change among individuals or groups, and how would such change be assessed?

• If we evaluate progress toward our objectives, who will do the evaluation and how will it be done? If objectives are not being reached, what action will be taken and by whom? Possibly even more challenging, if God blesses our effort, and our objectives and expectations are being met or exceeded, how do we share the credit? Who can say what to whom? And, is there a need for us all to agree on how various partners will publicize the success in each one's information/promotion programs?

• Do we share common expectations? Quite apart from our formal objectives, do we, as leaders, have other expectations? When we ask the question, "What is the absolute minimum that I am praying will be realized in this partnership?" what is the answer—and what does the answer really mean?

• How do we see the timetable or schedule for the work? Why is a timetable important for this project or partnership? What are the implications if we miss our schedule? Who will be affected and how, and what is likely to happen if the schedule has to be changed?

• What about policies or procedures related to administration and finance? Again, taking the time to talk through in *detail* the expectations that *each of us has* is critical. Matters such as project supervision, personnel recruiting, administration, evaluation, project reporting, basis for financial contributions and/or obligations, and length of term for the project all deserve careful, prayerful consideration *before* we start the project.

Lack of Effective Communications

If we have taken the time to work through the above issues, we are well on our way. However, one thing is clear: it takes not only energy and vision to *start* a partnership—it takes a major, conscious commitment to *maintain* a healthy partnership.

This suggests that we must make a specific commitment to how often we will communicate, about what topics, for what purpose—and *who will have the responsibility for making sure the communication occurs.*

One of the most overlooked communication issues is the fact that ministry partnerships usually have at least four constituencies—each of them with their needs, each deserving special communications consideration.

- First, there is the audience we are trying to reach for Christ or to serve in His name.

- Then, there is the staff and management of each "partner ministry." They must regularly ask themselves, "How does this partnership support our mission objectives?"

- Beyond these, there is the praying and giving constituency at home, who have made the resources available that are being used every day in the partnership. They want and deserve information about how their "investments" are being used and what the return on investment is.

- Finally, the partnership itself—the group of ministries that have come together for some common objectives. They develop expectations, hopes, and dreams—collectively.

Effective communications with all of these constituencies is vital.

Personality Conflicts

Effective partnerships are unlikely to form and certainly cannot long survive when serious personality conflicts exist between leaders or other team members among the partner ministries. We have been involved in some partnerships where prayer and personal reconciliation were the only way forward in the partnership. There was no point in trying to deal with practical project matters if deep personality problems or conflicts were being overlooked or not dealt with.

This is one of the areas where true partnership is a refining fire that few other Christian experiences provide. There *must* be a climate of trust and openness for partnerships to function effectively, to last long enough to have real impact, and to provide the power of credibility of the gospel.

For many people, both Western and non-Western individuals, this type of tough love is just that—difficult. However, it is a love that is born out of simultaneous commitment to the individuals involved in conflict as well as to the testimony of Christ's Kingdom. Without this sensitive yet active role of reconciliation, the prospect for lasting partnerships is hopeless.

> *One partnership in a particularly difficult region had been in development for over two years. However, a cloud hung over the process in the form of broken relationships, personality conflicts, and a lack of trust. When the formation meetings were actually held, all-night prayer and reconciliation meetings were as essential a part of the process as were the daytime meetings dealing with practical ministry matters.*

Partnerships: Challenges for the '90s

Those of us involved in missions and evangelism in the '90s will be stretched beyond our imagination as we face new circumstances and new opportunities. For these circumstances, partnerships can provide us with a tool kit diverse in strength, flexible in character, economical in implementation, and powerful in spiritual potential.

Choosing to ignore the signs of change and the remarkable opportunities that come with such change can be fatal for a ministry.

But what are some of the circumstances that will deserve (if not demand) new forms of ministry collaboration? Here are four issues suggestive of the future.

Massive Shift in Population

Populations will shift from the rural areas to the increasingly dense, seemingly out-of-control, urban centers of the world. The megacities and their smaller yet similar look-alikes. The great centers of despair, frustration, and strife, where local governments and other social structures are increasingly incapable of delivering solutions.

By 2000 there will be over 500 cities with populations of over one million. Twenty-five cities will be over 10 million. Every one of these cities deserves a strategic evangelism partnership with the full complement of Kingdom resources consciously and prayerfully focused through a diversified yet coordinated evangelization strategy.

Radical Political Changes

Radical political changes such as we have seen in former Marxist areas highlight the need for flexible, more fully coordinated Kingdom resources. In the wake of these changes, there are rising concerns over duplication of ministry effort and, in some cases, over blatant opportunism in the former Soviet Union. Often the local churches have not been taken into account and have suffered rather than being encouraged. And major Western funding sources are increasingly frustrated over the apparent unwillingness of Western ministries to invest the time and effort to coordinate their activities—particularly in the European areas of what is now the CIS.

In the meantime, outreach to the over 60 million people in the Islamic areas of the old Soviet Union is still comparatively modest, thus providing a unique opportunity for collaboration in partnership over the next few years.

What will happen in places like China, Burma, and areas like Cambodia, Laos, and Vietnam as the winds of political change continue to blow? Will we continue to work individualistically, dissipating resources and reducing effectiveness? Or will we, right now, begin active work to pray and talk together, to develop new alliances, new forms of partnership—preparing for these changing circumstances?

Financial Resources

Financial resources required for rapidly expanding ministry will place demands never dreamed of before on Christian organizations. Changing international political circumstances mean ministry opportunities are expanding at unprecedented speed. At the same time, the funding of non-Westerners, soon to be the *majority* of our missionary personnel, will become more and more challenging. Two Thirds World countries, deeply in debt, and Western countries with seemingly less and less to spend on more and more, provide a financial complexity never before known in missions. What can be done *now* to creatively joint venture the funding needed for Kingdom witness through partnerships?

Organizational and Structural Changes

Radical organizational and structural changes of the postmodern era may be the most daunting challenge for missionary efforts in the next decade. The signs are everywhere. International business may be showing the way, but wide-awake mission leaders have seen the trends for some time.

A high percentage of Western mission agencies are still struggling with top-down, more traditional hierarchies—both within their own administration and as they try to link with other agencies. There still seems to be difficulty in moving to more widely distributed, bottom-up, participative decision-making. The "flatter" organizations of the future will be highly flexible, oriented around specific, limited objectives. They will be able to attract and motivate individuals, as well as have the sense of identity yet flexibility that will allow them to know where they can make specific contributions—*while linking with other ministries of like mind.*

In further examples of these structural changes, mission agencies are already feeling the effect of the "ad hocracies" within the church—self-forming clusters of initiative and new types of coalitions undertaking ministry. Local churches, in many cases with budgets larger than more than 50 percent of all mission societies, are rapidly emerging as direct players on the international missions scene. In some cases they are forming their own partnerships in the "home country" and linking directly with projects in the field. In other cases, they are linking directly with partnerships in the field—looking every bit like another mission agency in their own right.

Then, in the new order of things there is the decline of missionary candidates for a high percentage of Western mission societies—part of the fallout of shifting values, perceptions, and resulting new structures. At the same time, young, current generation, specialized, sharply focused, *new* mission societies are emerging, proliferating, and attracting candidates in large numbers.

I am firmly convinced that most traditional mission agencies that cannot sharply rethink both their mission and structures, finding new ways to collaborate with the church at home and other missions in the field, are doomed to disappear over the next 10 to 15 years. In the past, our individualism may have been justified as perceived uniqueness of vision or fear of loss of identity. It may have been thinly disguised pride in "doing it alone." Whatever the reason, isolation will, in the end, be the death of such ministries.

> *One partnership had a working group focused on a minority language of the region. Forming an ad hoc committee with no constitution, operating only by consensus and regular inter-mission reporting, the group facilitated New Testament translations, "Jesus" film productions, radio programs, and other innovations. And, their collective effort brought in over $600,000 annually in new funds that were not available before. Despite controversy and resistance from the "we've never done it that way" crowd, a major evangelical denominational mission agency spawned two trend-setting programs—each with its own leadership. In both cases the programs were designed to respond to new circumstances: the need for creative access to difficult political areas and the need to mobilize resources from whatever evangelical quarter and to partner with others for evangelization of unreached people.*

Final Thoughts

If everything else is forgotten, here is my list of essentials for effective partnership:

1. Partnerships need individuals of vision and influence who champion the idea in the beginning and continue to be strong advocates in their own ministry and in the larger coalition. Without people of vision and commitment, partnerships perish.

2. Lasting, effective partnerships take time to develop. They are a process, not an event. If you call a formation or even exploratory meeting too early, in the process you will likely kill the possibility of a partnership. Ultimately what is required in partnerships is trust. Take the time to establish it, privately and then later in a group, and it will pay you rich dividends.

3. Lasting partnerships need a facilitator—someone who, by consensus, has been given the role of keeping the fires burning. Most serious partnerships have a facilitator working half to full time, loaned or seconded by a visionary ministry. Prophet, servant, coordinator, and resource person, this facilitator has to be trained and nurtured. Serving everyone in a partnership is often a unique, lonely task.

4. Partnerships must have clear, well-defined objectives: limited and realistic in the beginning, more expansive as the group experiences success. Participating partner agencies must likewise have clear mission statements and live by them. Otherwise they will never understand how their role in the partnership "fits." Frustration will be the sure result.

5. Realistic partnerships understand the four constituencies and plan to meet their needs. There are many more players around the table at any partnership meeting than we often acknowledge—or remember. Forget them and eventually the partnership will fail.

6. Long-term, effective partnerships are tough to start. They take a long time and are energy intensive in the start-up phases. But, like any effort, the real test is long-term maintenance; making sure the vision stays alive, the focus is clear,

communications are good, and people and ministries are fulfilled. Getting a marriage started is difficult enough. Having one that lasts 25-30 years and that is still fulfilling and joyful is an awesome challenge.

7. Effective partnerships expect problems and change and plan ahead for them. Make sure you have built into the process a means for dealing with changes, exceptions, disappointments, unfulfilled commitments, and simply the unexpected. A wise man knows one thing—the only predictable thing is change.

8. Partnerships are more than coordination, planning, strategies, and tactics. Ultimately ours is a gospel of restored relationships. Effective partnerships understand this and spend time actively building and maintaining relationships of trust and concern. Good communications, prayer for one another (not just for high-sounding ministry issues), and sharing experiences like the communion table—which has a uniquely powerful ability to bind us together and to Christ—all contribute.

9. Effective partnerships spend more time on clarifying the vision, objectives, and identifying resources for their common concerns than they do on organizational structure. If you can do it by consensus, do not write a constitution!

10. Understand that partnerships do not come free. Just participating in planning and coordination take your time and some of your budget. But also understand that, having made that investment, you should be able to identify "returns" that you could never have realized going it alone.

The "old order" of Jesus' day, both Jews and Gentiles, wondered at the new order that was established because of the cross and the resurrection—all testified to by the changed lives of the new believers and the obvious, profound, life-changing effect of the message on their *relationships*.

May the Father's love, Christ's sacrifice, and the indwelling power of the Holy Spirit renew our communities in the same manner.

> *"As, therefore, God's picked representatives of the new humanity... let the peace of Christ rule in your hearts, remembering that as members of one body you are called to live in harmony, and never forget to be thankful for what God has done for you."*
>
> — *Colossians 3:12a, 15 (Phillips)*

Phill Butler, a North American, served as an ABC News international correspondent, built and managed several commercial radio stations. In 1967 he founded Intercristo, a computer-based clearinghouse for Christian work opportunities, serving as its president until 1979; he established Interdev in 1974, and has served as the Chairman of the WEF Communications Training Group, and as the Director of the 1974 Lausanne Communications program. He has published widely on the subject of communications, world missions, and partnership. Interdev's prime focus is on developing international strategic evangelism partnerships. Mr. Butler is married to Sybil Stanton and has two grown daughters. He is a consultant to the WEF Missions Commission.

3

Responding to Butler: Mission in Partnership

R. Theodore Srinivasagam

When two or more people agree to work together for a common purpose, it is partnership. This is true not only for individuals, but also for a variety of enterprises, organizations, churches, and missions too. Most of us would agree that partnerships are necessary in missions today as we face the enormous task of reaching the unreached and building the church.

As we look at the Bible, the principles of partnership are brought out again and again. God created man to live in fellowship with Him and in partnership with other people. Adam and Eve were to live in partnership, the tribes of Israel were to work in partnership, the disciples of Jesus were to function in partnership, the churches were to grow in partnership, and missionary enterprise was to be accomplished in partnership.

Phillip Butler has ably brought out various aspects of motivation for partnership from Scripture, world conditions, and mission effectiveness. But as he has emphasized, it is good to look at the practical aspects of partnership.

Missionary work today is not done in isolation. There are churches, or at least Christians, in most countries of the world, whether weak or strong. So churches and mission agencies that send out missionaries have to relate to them. Further, during the past 30 years God has raised many mission agencies in the Two Thirds World which have sent several thousands of missionaries across cultural barriers. For this reason, missionaries of different agencies, church backgrounds, and nationalities need to relate to each other effectively.

Types of Partnership

Partnership relationships have been in existence for a long time, some actively fostered and others in benign neglect. There are basically two types of partnerships.

1. Partnership in Isolation

This type of partnership appears contradictory in terms, but it can be seen all around us. This is a partnership in which each mission or church does its own work, perhaps in its own area, but without a close link with others. Some of these partnerships are as follows:

• Geographical comity arrangements.

• Church/mission agreements, where the church emerged out of an older mission agency's church planting ministry.

• Associations of like-minded churches and mission agencies.

2. Partnership in Dynamic Relationships

The partners in this kind of partnership are dynamically related to each other, both in terms of geographical location and tasks to be performed. This partnership is entered into for more effective ministry. Following are some of the areas for this type of partnership:

• Reaching target groups of people.

• Reaching target areas that have opened up recently.

- Performing target tasks together.

Partnership that is dynamic can be structured in the two ways mentioned by Phillip Butler. The future of missions will perhaps be based on networks.

- Bilateral partnership—Where one agency links up with another. This is easier to develop than multi-agency partnerships.

- Multilateral partnership—Where several agencies link up together for a common task.

Functioning of These Partnerships

These partnerships can function in two ways, as explained by Phillip Butler in his paper.

1. Horizontally Integrated Network

In this arrangement, different groups of people from different agencies work together for a common goal such as Bible translation, a literacy program, a tuberculosis eradication scheme, or a particular project. In India we have seen this taking place effectively for more than 10 years in training and guiding Indian Bible translators in unwritten languages. The Indian Institute of Cross-Cultural Communication (IICCC), established under the Indian Missions Association (IMA), was jointly set up by several mission agencies for training Bible translators in India. Indian mission agencies and churches involved in Bible translation and literacy work send their workers for this training and also obtain consultant help. Most of the teachers come from SIL, IEM, FMPB, IEHC, etc. The Bible Society of India is involved in printing and distribution of translated Scriptures. This partnership has encouraged many new agencies and churches to think in terms of recruiting workers for this work, as well as encouraging the whole task of Bible translation in India.

2. Vertically Integrated Network

In this arrangement, different groups of people from different agencies work together to reach a particular group of unreached people. Several missions are doing this within their own ranks. For example, in the Indian Evangelical Mission (IEM) we have teams of missionaries trying to reach target groups of people. There are church planters, medical workers, Bible translators, literacy workers, and those involved in development projects among a tribal people in Andhra Pradesh and among the Kukna tribal people in the Dangs District of Gujarat.

We have also seen multiple agencies working together effectively. In reaching the Korku tribal people of Maharashtra and Madhya Pradesh, we have a partnership agreement between the Baptist Mission in Central India, the Zoram Baptist Mission of Mizoram, and the IEM. The main Bible translation work into the Korku language has been assigned to the IEM. Literature can be produced by all groups and distributed into all the areas. The church structure is under the direction of the Baptist Church. The leaders meet periodically to pray and plan the work and to allocate various ministries. The missionaries of all the partner agencies meet together for a time of Bible study, prayer, and interaction at least once a year. This partnership has enriched and encouraged all the agencies involved.

These kinds of dynamic partnerships have also been established between church and mission agency, church and church for missionary work, mission agency and mission agency, etc. Further, these partnerships can also be between Western and non-Western partners. The IEM has partnership arrangements with some international mission agencies such as the Overseas Missionary Fellowship (OMF) for work in East Asia, with Interserve for work in areas of West Asia, and with SIM for work in some countries of Africa and South America. In all these cases, IEM missionaries who fit the norms of partner missions are seconded to the mission agencies to work in other countries and reach particular groups of people that have been mutually targeted. They are full members of the partner missions as well and come under their direction and supervision on the field. Their expenses while outside India are taken care of by the partner missions. When the missionaries return to India on home assignment, they are taken care of by IEM and also come under the direction of IEM. We have also had three-way partnerships in which a church seconds a missionary to IEM, and IEM in turn places the missionary with a partner mission in another country and vice versa. We have found if the guidelines have been worked out properly, partnership arrangements work satisfactorily.

Areas and Tasks That Will Benefit From Partnership Arrangements

There are many tasks that stand neglected because of lack of suitable personnel or financial resources by any one agency. However, if several agencies having similar or common goals join together, these tasks can be done. Some of the areas and tasks which need such cooperative efforts, especially among Two Thirds World missions, are as follows:

1. *Survey and research.* These tasks can be in areas of locating and describing unreached people groups, providing insights from case studies from the field, population trends, new openings for work, etc.

2. *Training.* Training tasks can include developing missionary training institutes to equip national missionaries, developing training programs for new Christians, sending suitably qualified personnel for teaching and training, etc.

3. *Projects.* Several projects such as community health work, Bible translation, literacy, and various development activities need specialized skills.

4. *Pioneering into new areas or specific groups of people.* Agencies from both the West and the non-Western world can join together to develop work in newly opened countries and specific people groups.

5. *Communication skills.* In developing indigenous communication methods as well as in enhancing production of

literature and mass media, joint efforts are needed, since many non-Western churches and agencies lack the skills which can be imparted by Western colleagues.

Accomplishing the Tasks

There are two ways that the tasks identified above can be accomplished:

1. Sharing of Resources

This includes all kinds of resources that the partner mission agencies have and are willing to share.

Personnel

Experts available from one agency can be seconded to another for work on the common task. These tasks can be both short term and long term. In countries where long-term visas are hard to obtain, short-term workers with necessary abilities are very useful, especially in areas of teaching, training, administrative work, medical work, etc. There can also be exchange of personnel between agencies in these and other areas. IEM's training program called the Outreach Training Institute near Bangalore has benefited from such teaching personnel from other countries.

Proper Use of Property and Facilities

In many places there are properties and facilities that are not used properly, or are underused. These can be shared for a common goal.

Funding

This is a sensitive issue and is one of the most difficult areas of partnership. This requires trust and accountability. There are generally three types of funding relationships:

- Sharing of personnel only without any provision of funds.
- Sharing of funds only without any sharing of personnel.
- Sharing of both personnel and funds (partial or full).

The agencies concerned need to work out which is the best type of relationship for them.

2. Task-Oriented Partnerships

In missionary enterprise there are many tasks which can be done more effectively by cooperative enterprise than by any one single agency. So task-oriented partnerships can be developed. In several places cooperative evangelism, radio work, medical work, child care work, and development work have been done in this way.

Issues and Problems in Partnership

One should recognize that there will be problems in any kind of partnership, depending upon the people involved, organizational structure, perception of benefits that will accrue, etc. Partnership will also raise new issues as the partnership progresses.

Phillip Butler has pointed out a few problem areas in his paper:

1. *Cultural differences.* Many misunderstandings develop because perceptions differ not only between Western and non-Western agencies, but also between different cultural groups within Asia and even within a country.

2. *Lack of effective communication.* This can become a problem if there are no clear guidelines as to whom one should communicate, and also if English is going to be the language of communication but one of the partners is limited in that language.

3. *Personality conflicts.* Personal equations play a major role in fostering relationships, especially in the Two Thirds World. Emphasis needs to be given to resolve these conflicts.

Certain other problems and issues may also develop. Some of these are as follows:

1. Lack of clarity in guidelines and purpose of partnership when partnerships are formed in haste.

2. Unwillingness to release personal identity in working towards a common task and not providing the resources needed.

3. Lack of visible results to enthuse the supporting constituency.

4. Lack of trust and accountability.

5. Unequal partnership arrangements.

6. Tendencies towards dependency on one partner for the development of the agreed task, with other partner or partners slowly withdrawing.

7. Organizational structure of partner agencies not being flexible enough for the work to move forward.

8. Inability or unwillingness of grassroots level workers to make the partnership successful, even though leadership may be enthusiastic.

9. Division in leadership of one partner agency, leading to non-implementation of the task or hindering the task.

10. Lack of accurate reporting, evaluation, and follow-up action.

Some Specific Issues
in Partnership Relationships

Church/Parachurch Partnership Relationships

These issues have been discussed in many forums, and tension between them continues in many situations. For effective partnership between church and parachurch agencies, all players need to understand their roles and limitations. Very often the church is perceived to be slow and not capable of meeting the various needs which the parachurch agencies, by concentrating on specific ministries, are able to meet. On the other hand, parachurch agencies are looked upon as unaccountable to the church and often have their roots or draw their resources from foreign soil. In spite of these and other misunderstandings, effective partnerships need to be worked out, however long they may take, as the totality of ministry will benefit from this effort.

Church/Mission Agency Partnership Relationships

There are several aspects here:

1. Many churches sacrificially give of their finances and qualified personnel to mission agencies so that the gospel can be taken to peoples and areas where the church is unable to go or supervise its personnel. This in turn requires that mission agencies, especially interdenominational agencies, give accurate reports of the ministry, as well as be accountable to the church for the finances they receive from it. When these things do not happen, the church feels neglected and friction develops. So these relationships that are formed should be guarded and nurtured with care. In churches having their own denominational mission boards, this is taken care of by the mission board structures.

2. When missionaries are sent to work in a cross-cultural situation, it is essential that the mission agency concerned take into consideration all aspects of the work in order to develop a partnership relationship with a nearby church or denomination. This will avoid various misunderstandings. The Indian Evangelical Mission has followed this procedure in its various mission fields and has partnership arrangements with the concerned dioceses of the Church of South India, the Church of North India, the Methodist Church in India, and the Baptist Churches. Other mission agencies also have developed similar partnership agreements.

3. In recent times, some local churches are directly sending and supervising their missionaries. In such cases, very often the onus of developing good working partnerships in the places of ministry falls on the missionaries themselves. Therefore, they need guidance.

Donor/Recipient Partnership Relationships

The major area which causes friction between donors and recipients in this kind of partnership is finance. The following issues need to be understood and dealt with:

1. Accountability by the recipient partner for the funds provided by the donor.

2. Donors dictating unhelpful or unworkable terms or trying to direct the work, such as:

   • Changing the structure of the organization or project.

   • Demanding data or information which, when given and publicized, can hinder and/or damage the work.

3. Finances given by donors for needs as perceived by the donor but not meeting the real needs of the partner and the ministry.

4. Submission of reports by the recipient partner and production of publicity materials by the donor which are less than honorable.

5. Development of a patron-dependent relationship.

Credible Partnership Relationships

In these days there is increasing desire to find partners both among Western and non-Western missions and churches. Non-Western agencies are seeking help from the West, and Western agencies want to find partners from the Two Thirds World who will produce the desired results for their financial investment and other input. Credibility suffers in many cases. There are churches and agencies in the West who have funded projects and programs of one kind or another in the Two Thirds World, but are not able to receive any reports or results of their funding. In some cases, neither the projects nor the recipients are traceable! In other cases, because of the pressure brought about by funding agencies and churches (both Western and affluent Two Thirds World) and out of fear of losing their support, the recipient agencies have "produced" baptisms, new churches, hostels for children, etc.! Sometimes whole congregations have been taken over because of the power of money. As a result of such situations, the credibility of partner agencies must be assessed before agreements are reached. National evangelical fellowships and national mission associations can provide counsel in this matter, and their assistance should be sought.

Middle Person as Broker in Partnership Relationships

Apart from direct negotiations between partner agencies from different cultural backgrounds or between Western and non-Western partnerships, a "middle person" can smooth out the path. A person who is familiar with the partners can help by asking the right questions of the partners concerned and can also find answers. In addition, he can discern the real attitudes the potential partners have towards each other.

Developing Partnerships

Getting a partnership started and developed takes time, effort, and willingness on the part of the individuals concerned. Partnership is like a journey with partners traveling together. The more they do things together, the more likely they will understand each other better. In these days of "instant" things, it is good to remember that a good, healthy, long-lasting, and fruitful partnership takes time. In the missionary enterprise, such a partnership brings glory to God.

Missionary work cannot be done today in isolation. The goal of both churches and missions around the world, whether from the West or the non-Western world, is the same. Missionary work has to be done in partnership, and partnerships need to be developed much further than they are at present. Doors that may be closed for personnel of some countries may be open to others, and we need to develop mechanisms for mutual support—between churches and mission agencies of the West and those in the Two Thirds World, for the common purpose of being obedient to God's commission. Personnel of one country can be supported by churches and mission agencies of another country for the ministry of the gospel in a third country. Other dynamic partnerships should be developed, by having truly international and interracial teams working together as a witness to the world. Cannot finances of one country be used for projects of another for the sake of fulfilling the missionary mandate? Cannot missionaries from the Two Thirds World minister to the growing immigrant communities in the Western world supported by the churches in the West?

It must realized that the future of missions will perhaps be based on the formation of both national and international networks. It should also be remembered that both established missions and churches and emerging missions and churches are not self-sufficient. We need each other to fulfill the Great Commission given by our Lord Jesus Christ. May such partnerships blossom and, as a consequence, may this earth be filled with the glory of God as the waters cover the sea.

An Indian citizen, Theodore Srinivasagam earned his Ph.D. in marine biology from Madras University, served as a professor, and completed further research in the UK, where he received direction for his future life work. Upon returning to India, he was seconded by the Indian Evangelical Mission to the OMF and sent to Thailand to work with university students in Bangkok. Due to visa difficulties, he was forced to return to India and began his leadership role in IEM. He succeeded Theodore Williams as General Secretary of IEM in 1990. He is married and lives in Bangalore.

4

Responding to Butler:
Reflections From Europe

Stanley Davies

I welcome Phill Butler's paper for its breadth and insights into this vital subject of building effective partnerships in world mission. I appreciate the way he differentiates between the different kinds of partnerships and the practical steps he indicates are necessary to implement effective partnerships.

Specific Responses

In response, I would first like to comment on specific points Phill Butler makes in his paper.

1. I was surprised at the "almost complete lack of significant comment about theological issues as a recurring problem in partnerships." Is this because any of the partnerships so far entered into are only with those of identical doctrinal positions? I think this is likely. However, I am aware of several initiatives in the Middle East that are exploring partnerships between evangelical mission agencies and some of the historic churches of that region. I cannot imagine that theological problems have not arisen in the exploration of such partnerships.

In a similar vein, I am aware that at the International Charismatic Conference on World Evangelization that took place in Brighton, England, in July 1991, various difficult theological issues were either subsumed because of a common acceptance of a certain position relating to pneumatology, or were ignored as being too divisive for such a conference to handle.

2. The observation that "almost none of the Western respondents indicated any direct role for the Western churches in partnerships" would suggest that the wrong group of Western leaders were asked the question. Most Western mission leaders only report on their own activities in such a questionnaire. If Western denominational leaders or ministers of megachurches in the West had been asked, I suspect you would have had a different answer.

3. I believe that vertically integrated partnerships are a real breakthrough that the Lord has given to us for this period of mission activity around the world.

4. Phill Butler writes about the heavy influence of individualism in Western agencies. I see this as a scourge of Western Christianity. The Western culture that has spawned this type of excessive individualism is infecting and affecting many relationships within missions, as well as the way Western missions view the possibility of partnerships with non-Western agencies.

Talking recently at the European EMA meetings, our German brethren spoke with sadness about the proliferation of one man/one family mission groups in Germany that appear to have little inclination to work with other groups.

One very positive aspect of the new churches movement in Europe has been a recovery of the need for community, with its emphasis on fellowship and the life of the body of believers. This is a revolt from the evils of excessive individualism that is a concern eating at the heart of Western culture.

5. One of Butler's titles is called "Mission Effectiveness." I strongly believe that too many agencies are unwilling to attempt to measure effectiveness. Many missionaries are threat-

ened with talk of "evaluation." Many missions need to measure their effectiveness in the light of the investment that the people of God provide for their programs. This will also be necessary in assessing the effectiveness of partnerships.

6. Phill Butler touches the nerve when he writes of "personality conflicts." I believe that we need to emphasize that spiritual gifting alone for service is not enough. Spiritual grace and fruit are essential for lasting and effective ministry, as well as for enabling partnerships to come into being and prosper.

There is no substitute for Christlike character and holiness of life in the servants of God who are involved in mission. I tremble as I think of the tragedies I have had to deal with over the past three years when ministries and partnerships have been almost destroyed by personality conflicts.

7. A reference is made to some local churches with budgets larger than more than 50 percent of all mission societies. Do we have any representatives of these mega-churches here? Is this a phenomenon only limited to the USA? If not, we must give serious attention as to how to involve them in these discussions.

8. I fully endorse the section that states that "most traditional mission agencies that cannot sharply rethink both their mission and structures… are doomed to disappear over the next 10 to 15 years." There is an urgent need to find new ways to collaborate with the church at home and with other missions in the field.

From a UK perspective, I can underline the fact that only those agencies that are prepared to adapt to a changing world are prospering. Some, sadly, have failed to realize the changes and are becoming fossilized.

9. The final section stating the essentials is a most valuable checklist on making partnerships work.

Additional Observations

I want to move on to make a few additional observations about interdependent partnerships.

1. "There is nothing more interesting, exasperating, and exciting than partnership." So wrote Maurice Sinclair in his excellent book *Ripening Harvest, Gathering Storm.* All of us who have entered into any kind of partnership can identify with these words. But have we the necessary patience and humility to implement effective partnerships? One of the problems of Western mission agencies is the insatiable desire for "results." Requests for success stories for the home constituency can be a snare. How can you write home about the hours, days, or weeks spent in hammering out global partnerships? Will they understand? Will they appreciate their importance?

2. Part of the difficulty in entering into effective partnerships is the need to face up to the key issues of power and authority. I was surprised that Phill Butler hardly touched on this subject. Understanding who makes decisions and how they are made is fundamental to an effective partnership. Without clarity here, the prospect of any lasting partnership is slim.

Determining the level of decision making is essential. This is a current issue being debated in the European Community. Where should decisions about national sovereignty be taken?

In the political field, the debate is between London, Paris, or Rome on the one hand, or Brussels or Strasburg on the other. In the mission world, the debate is between Pasadena, Wheaton, London, or Stuttgart on the one hand, and Nairobi, São Paulo, Seoul, or Bangalore on the other.

Is the decision-making process governed by Roberts Rules or the Westminster debating pattern on the one hand, or on the basis of mutual submission, earnest intercession, and consensus agreement on the other?

3. "Interdependent partnerships will be characterized by reconciliation, understanding, mutuality, and often suffering." If we are prepared to pay the price, then we can expect to see

the Lord's blessing on such partnerships. I believe that one of the greatest hindrances to effective partnerships often centers around the issue of finance. We cannot avoid facing up to the thorny problems of differentials in standards of living and of working out methods of accountability for funds donated to projects or partnerships.

4. In the last two or three years, the Evangelical Alliance in the UK has developed a close partnership with the Afro-Caribbean Evangelical Alliance. Close working partnerships are also being developed between the Evangelical Alliance, the Evangelical Missionary Alliance, and Tear Fund with the exploration of a number of exciting joint projects. One of these is the development of the Rapid Response to Major Disasters project. Over 50 agencies are now on the Register. The project's aim is to set in place a network of UK agencies that can be activated very quickly when a major disaster strikes anywhere in the world. Eight Regional Coordinators have been appointed with their deputies to call an information-sharing meeting of those agencies involved in the stricken area. Many of those agencies already work in partnership with national churches on all continents. It is our hope that this initiative will be duplicated in other countries. The UK no longer thinks it has all the answers to this world's needs!

5. In Europe there is a growing recognition that new forms of partnership are needed to re-evangelize our continent. New "Macedonian Calls" are being sounded in different countries of Europe to "come over and help us." The requests are not only to engage in evangelism among the diverse immigrant populations from Africa and Asia, but also to reach the resistant Caucasian majority who have been hardened against the gospel by secularism and materialism. Some are turning to occultism and the New Age philosophies. We need help in demonstrating the power of the gospel, as well as in proclaiming it to a new generation of Europeans.

6. May the triune God—Father, Son, and Holy Spirit—enable us to work together with Him as well as with one another in effective partnerships that will clearly demonstrate the unity and diversity of the Christian faith in our needy world.

Stanley Davies is the General Secretary of the UK Evangelical Mission-
ary Alliance. He was born in India of missionary parents. For 15 years
he worked in Kenya with the Africa Inland Mission in a variety of
ministries. He is currently Vice Chairman of the WEF Missions Commis-
sion.

Part Two:
Critical Issues
in Partnerships

5

Cultural Issues
in Partnership in Mission

Patrick Sookhdeo

The relationship of gospel with culture has been an issue in the church of Jesus Christ since its inception. For the last few decades, culture has featured prominently on the missiological map. It holds a prominent place amongst the various component parts of mission. Considerable research and writing have been done on the subject of culture. The Willowbank Report on gospel and culture, the Fuller School of World Mission, and others have helped shape our understanding of culture.

The recognition of past mistakes, together with the exploration of new models involving cultural authenticity, have led us into a more positive climate. It is not my purpose therefore to go over old ground, but rather to move the debate forward.

I want to argue that we must go beyond dwelling on previous mistakes and the guilt of the past. To obtain a new perspective on our partnerships in mission, we should seek an alternative to a Marxist dialectic in our interpretation of the world and, in particular, remove the conflict element. Our conflict should never be with each other. The only conflict should be between biblical absolutes that exist in permanent conflict with the world, the flesh, and the devil.

I want to argue that, while recognizing the importance of culture in form and communication, it can no longer be the altar at which we worship, the interpreter of all that we do. We need to rediscover biblical values which we all share, which transcend culture, which affirm culture, and which judge culture. We need to rediscover our biblical identity as the children of God over against our cultural affinities. We need to rediscover our common calling, that is, the evangelization of the whole world, as opposed to self-imposed cultural limits. We need to consider biblical *koinonia*—partnership—and the principles that determine our working relationships, and then go on to consider other obstacles to misunderstanding and how they can be removed.

Global Village or Not?

Marshall McLuhan's concept of the global village, a world that is shrinking fast, linked by rapid communication to facilitate the interchange of ideas and culture worldwide, has turned out to have a serious flaw: the villagers do not want to live together. Ironically, the very communication that was expected to make the world one has merely served to make clear "the profound cultural, religious, and political schisms that partition the globe." As David Toop, writing in *The Times* (April 24, 1992) summarizes: "Earth may be a hamlet, electronically, but the villagers are still strangers."

The global village concept did help in the understanding of what became known as the "new international man"—in other words, a person who is able to transcend cultural differences; who is able to enter into different cultural experiences; who is able to share in the life, meaning, and significance of others' culture; who is able to identify not with one particular culture but rather with a multicultural framework of society. Such an individual is able to understand and affirm cultural difference and, at the same time, to move freely from one culture to another and to feel reasonably comfortable in whichever culture he finds himself.

But the opposite of this is seen in the atomizing of humanity, caused by secularism and Western individualism, as evidenced by the growing emphasis on ethnicity linked to religion, language, and land. This trend is seen, for example, in the former Soviet Union, as its constituent peoples take the first opportunity to divide into separate ethnic groups again and also in the current tragic conflict in Yugoslavia. This growing separation will quickly lead to alienation, with all the attendant dangers.

Yet there is a further group—those who are able to accept cultural diversity, yet at the same time value their own cultural identity. This is very much the position of the USA and its development of cultural, racial, and religious pluralism.

Amid such positions there is also a growing sense of interdependence. As citizens sharing a common planet, all that we do impacts each other. The decline of global resources, the growth of world population, and the effects of environmental problems all demonstrate that the part cannot exist separate from the whole. John Donne's famous statement that "no man is an island" is true in more senses than he probably imagined.

In such a situation, old terminologies are increasingly irrelevant and are being abandoned. For example, vocabulary that divides the world into First, Second, and Third Worlds loses its importance, and there are those who argue not only that the use of such terms should be abandoned, but also that the presuppositions behind the terms must be abandoned too if we are to move forward. For the terms not only continue to suggest paternalism, but also induce a sense of dependence and a sense of arrogance in the respective parts of the world.

In this context, it is important to note the effects that the collapse of Marxism and socialism will have on the world community. A new age of capitalism, with economics at the center, has dawned. In this new age, emerging economies as well as established economies will be looking for new bilateral relationships and joint ventures. For both recognize increasingly their need of each other. With such relationships, there will of necessity come new ideas emanating from a desire for growth and expansion. It is recognized that patterns of economic development are heavily influenced by cultural norm, whether they have their origin within that culture or have been imposed from outside by another culture.

Similarly, in education there are calls now for greater internationalization, for universities to develop links with overseas departments and engage in joint research projects. The same also applies increasingly in other fields.

With the entering of new bilateral relationships and joint ventures, both economic and educational, the Western capitalist basis that emphasizes efficiency, structures, management principles, and organizational skills will increasingly dictate patterns of relationship. For a developing country, survival is likely to involve great changes of customs, cultural norms, and religious practices. A price may well have to be paid for these changes in the form of growing fundamentalism, which seeks to shape the future by returning to the past, covering not only religion, but also culture, values, etc.

Importance of Culture

Culture can be considered as all learned behavior, value systems, and social institutions. It is determined by the past, molded by present events, and affected by perceptions of the future.

Eugene Nida defines culture as all learned behavior which is socially acquired, that is, the material and non-material traits which are passed on from generation to generation.... They are both transmittable and accumulative.... Culture is an abstraction.... It is a way of behaving, thinking, and reacting.... We see the manifestation of culture in objects, actions, and situations.

While culture is important, we must go behind and beyond culture to feelings, emotions, aspirations, ambitions, and perceptions that all humanity shares. The Bible, though written over a period of more than a thousand years and in the context of various Middle Eastern cultures, yet remains relevant to every age of history, to every culture in the world, and to every situation people can enter. It is astonishingly relevant to every contemporary need. Its principles, founded on an unchanging God, are worked out in the context of change. It is a book about God and His dealing with human beings, who demonstrate a surprising commonness. The mistakes, the sins, the failures, as well as the successes and faithfulness of the saints of bygone ages, are not attributed to culture but rather to believers' relationship with God.

Culture affects behavior, and, as a result, behavior is all too often interpreted purely on the basis of culture. But for the Christian this can never be so, for behavior must ultimately be interpreted and determined by biblical values and norms. Righteousness and unrighteousness, holiness and sin, are not relative values rooted in culture, but absolutes. The way we treat each other, the way we behave, can never be seen as merely cultural.

None of us has truly New Testament culture. What we deem to be biblical is often born out of our socio-historical religious context. It is this that dictates and determines our patterns of behavior, the nature of our relationships, and the structures that we evolve. It is therefore important that we step back from our various socio-political and culturally interpreted contexts into the text and context of our Scriptures and use the principles contained there to guide and determine our way of life.

The Bible describes the pattern of relationships that ought to emerge, the attitudes that condition those relationships, and the actions that shape them.

A relationship:

- Must be entered into.
- Must be maintained.
- Involves growth and development.
- Adapts to changing situations.
- Must both give and receive.
- Involves mutual accountability.

- Must be open to correction.
- Must face the implicit as well as the explicit weaknesses of each other.

Relationships are the crux of *koinonia*—biblical fellowship and community—and it is on the concept of *koinonia* that a biblical understanding of partnership in mission is centered.

Partnership in Mission

1. We meet first as the people of God—Christians.

2. We serve a common Lord—Jesus Christ.

3. We share in a common purpose—mission—to establish the kingdom of God.

4. The sphere of our service is the world.

Christ calls His whole church to enter into His whole world to establish His kingdom. It is not our racial, cultural, educational, or economic characteristics that qualify us. Nor is it our identification with the race, culture, etc. of those to whom we minister that equips us. No part of the world is given to any group of people for them to exercise authority and responsibility over. Jehovah is not a tribal God. Although Paul was sent to the Gentiles and Peter to the Jews, neither claimed these peoples as their "private" mission field to the exclusion of all other workers. The church, the people of God, is not a tribal people. Our task is not a tribal task. We have a universal God, we are a universal people, and we a have a universal task.

There exists a contemporary danger of interpreting mission from within the historical cultural basis of society. Such a position can easily fall prey to a Marxist analysis: the conflict between the proletariat and the bourgeoisie. Analyses of mission in terms of conflict—for example, Western/non-Western or colonial/anti-colonial—are easily made, but it is essential that we go beyond the categories that have shaped contemporary history and arrive at a biblical position. This is not to underestimate or even to reject the existence of racism and paternalism during the past 200 years. Rather, it is to recognize the true identity we share. It was said of the children of

Israel that it was easier to get them out of Egypt than to get Egypt out of them. It is important that we recognize the deep sinfulness of mankind. Such an innate sinfulness is born out of self-interest. One facet of self-interest is the desire for self-preservation. This desire embraces the preservation not only of myself, but also of those who are close to my family and my community. It must be noted that there are positive aspects of self-interest, but when self-interest militates against the greater good of others, when others are sacrificed on the altar of self-interest, then it becomes sin. It is important that we recognize our common humanity in our creation and fall in Eden, our rebellion and subsequent diversity at Babel, our redemption at Calvary, and our new spiritual unity on the Day of Pentecost at Jerusalem. Tertullian described Christians as God's third race on earth, neither Jew nor Gentile, neither Greek nor barbarian, but God's new community here on earth.

With this in mind, we will now consider the principles and attitudes that affect our diversity.

Some New Definitions

Western society a generation ago was not so very dissimilar from many present-day non-Western cultures. For example, consider the importance of duty, loyalty, family, and honor. What we are reflecting on is not just the basic value systems of different cultures but the degree of change that has taken place to bring them to the point where they now are. Thus, to speak of non-Western cultures and Western culture is so broad a generalization as to be practically meaningless.

I would suggest another method of classifying culture:

1. Cultures that are still shaped by traditional values, including historic Christianity and other religious groupings.

2. Cultures that are shaped by Protestant values.

3. Cultures that have been shaped by contemporary secularism, which has its origin in industrialization and urbanization.

This classification of culture has important application in our interactions with each other. Much misunderstanding would be dispelled if only we could understand each other better. Furthermore, if we truly face up to the culturally related issues and the way we respond to them biblically, then the hurts and divisions that often occur may give way to peace and unity. In developing missiological partnerships, there are almost certain to be cultural differences; it is essential to be aware of these and to face them.

To take an example from the secular world, President Bush visited Japan last year to discuss bilateral trade agreements. When he left Japan he firmly believed that agreements had been made, only to discover that this was not the case. Various commentators suggested that the misunderstanding that occurred was because of an inability of each side to interpret the other side's culture in terms of what constituted a decision.

This issue often occurs when entering into missionary partnerships. Agreements, which for one culture may be regarded as sacrosanct and permanent, can in another culture be regarded as subject to adjustment depending on prevailing conditions. A clear example of this is the minutes of a meeting. In some cultures, minutes which have once been approved can never be changed, because they are a record of the past and the past cannot be changed. In another culture, minutes can be freely altered to correspond to what people would have said at the past meeting if they had known how the situation was going to develop at a later time.

In order to help develop better understanding in entering into missionary partnerships, I will now endeavor to touch on some of the specific cultural issues that can be a source of misunderstanding and conflict (these will be expressed in generalized terms).

Some Areas to Consider

1. In societies that are group-oriented as opposed to individualistic, where the extended family exists, leadership styles are often more paternalistic and even authoritarian in structure and style.

The family is effectively a social security and welfare system from the cradle to the grave. In this system, the wishes of the individual are subordinated to those of the family as a whole and in particular the eldest members of the family. The teacher or adviser is frequently regarded as a surrogate for the authority provided by the father. Hence, the individual finds it difficult to make decisions without direction from an approved authority source. In communication with others, he may need an "uncle" to convey his requests or plead his cause. In this situation, the "uncle" may well be manipulated. Also, the individual who succeeds, who "makes it," then has responsibility for the care and nurture of the other family members. Likewise, it is expected that the organization into which the individual enters will accept responsibility for the family members and even for future generations.

There are dangers here of nepotism and the development of dynastic leadership.

In contrast to this are societies where the needs and rights of the individual are paramount. These societies tend to lead to self-interest and utilitarianism, as other individuals are seen only in terms of what can be gained from them. They bring alienation among family members and lack any real understanding of community or of responsibility for others. Enjoyment has become one of the foundation stones of modern society. This value can easily spill over into the spiritual realm, where job satisfaction becomes the "be all and end all" of ministry. Duties and responsibilities are secondary. Great stress is laid on discovering one's own gifts and ministries. In such cultures, the gospel becomes entertainment, and service becomes self-fulfillment.

Again, prosperous societies tend to lay such a great emphasis on material wealth that their members find it difficult to relate to the poor and the weak and to exist alongside them. Missionaries who are used to a high standard of living find it difficult to become fully a part of the people, situations, and countries where such standards do not exist. This not only sets them apart but ultimately negates authentic incarnational mission.

2. A second important area is the relative emphasis laid on the personal and the institutional, on relationships and structures. There are those cultures that like to do things on a personal basis. They prefer to conduct their business with people whom they know and trust, and preferably on a face to face basis. The Western practice of communicating by circulating multiple copies of a letter, thus manipulating a situation to the disadvantage of the addressee, is not appropriate in such cultures. In these cultures, there do exist bureaucracies and impersonal institutions, but behind the facade of the institutions one finds business being done on a personal basis.

Obviously there are strengths and weaknesses to this system. The strengths are that if you have the right friends and contacts, strings can be pulled for you. If you need a job, you can always turn to someone on a personal basis; if you have a problem, you can visit someone with the ability to help or intercede, or telephone someone who will help you resolve the difficulty. There is an Arabic word *intisab* which roughly translated means "pull." It is the way in which things have been done for centuries in the Middle East and one which is highly regarded.

The weaknesses in this type of system include the self-selective element in terms of individuals with whom business is done. Confidentiality can easily lead to corruption. Lack of accountability makes the system open to abuse. Lack of adequate documentation can lead to misunderstanding and to the charge of changing the terms of reference to one's own advantage.

In the West, such a term as *intisab* with the above implications has a negative connotation. It implies deceitfulness, dishonesty, and manipulation. There is an Urdu proverb from Pakistan which says: "Because I have neither influence, bribe, nor relatives, my work will not prosper [I will not get ahead or get advancement]." In Urdu, the word for influence is *rasuch*, bribe is *rishuat*, and the term for relatives is *rishdadari*. The common sound of the first syllable links the three ideas. (A certain Christian leader from the developing world, who in his inaugural address declared that he would not accept the pressures that came from these three areas, was forced out of office in less than a year because of his inability to conform to what was required by the Christian community.) In the West, such contacts are rare and their use is regarded as suspect. Part of the reason for this understanding lies in the way things are done. In the West, procedure determines practice and takes precedence over relationships. The emphasis is on institutions and on standardization through filling in endless forms and feeding endless computers. Yet the impersonality that may seem to many an obvious weakness is at the same time a safeguard to ensure propriety, honesty, fair dealing, and even-handedness.

3. Another cultural contrast is found between appearances and reality. In some cultures, good interpersonal relationships take precedence over competence and efficiency. To get along with a person with the minimum of friction is more important than the rate at which the job is done. To minimize confrontation or abrasiveness is essential. In other cultures, abrasive and aggressive behavior can be tolerated and even encouraged to some extent if such behavior leads to increased competence and efficiency, although too much of it will also be penalized.

The desire to be non-confrontational can lead to dishonesty in relationships, for it can inhibit open and frank discussion. A desire to maintain good relationships at any cost can lead to denial of truth and an unwillingness to face up to wrongdoing. The desire to save the face of the other person can mean there is no system of drawing attention to mistakes and correcting them. Peer pressure and the need to conform to societal norms are more powerful influences than conscience and truth.

In the Japanese language, a distinction is made between the private face and the public face. The private face, *honne*, describes true intention, real meaning, and true motive. The public face is described by the word *tatemae*, meaning structure or framework and thence facade, appearance, show. Such a distinction between private and public face is not limited to Japan but can be found in many other cultures where it may not be so consciously articulated and defined.

4. An important point to note has to do with those whose own cultural make-up is not "pure" but a mixture of a number of cultures. This complicates the process of seeking to understand them. Those from the developing world who are trained in the West, and particularly in the USA, Britain, Germany, and Holland, tend to learn the subculture peculiar to their country of training. The more one knows about a person's background, the better one can accurately interpret what that person says and does and the better one can predict how the person will respond in the future.

Building Biblical Relationships Across Cultures

Biblical relationships are to be founded on biblical values. This means that truth, accountability, integrity, authority, and loyalty are not to be interpreted as cultural variables but should be founded on eternal principles. For example—truth. The legal requirement for "the truth, the whole truth, and nothing but the truth" is founded on the biblical position that there should be no deception, whether by commission or by omission.

Another example is reliability and accuracy. Jesus counseled: "Let your yes be yes and your no be no" (Matt. 5:37). Christians should be trustworthy in all that they say and all that they undertake to do.

The Christian life is to be marked by a fundamental loyalty to Christ, His Word, and His kingdom. All other loyalties are secondary. We are Christians first and everything else second.

It has been said that in Islam all relationships are based on mistrust. Too often this has also become the case among Christians. Mistrust occurs both within cultures (for example, among Christians in the Muslim world) and cross-culturally (for example, Western missions mistrusting national Christians and failing to establish relationships with them).

If as Christians we are to enter into meaningful partnership relationships with each other, then this will involve a whole new way of thinking and behaving. It will demand of us a trust and an openness such as we have not previously seen. It will require us to break out of our respective cultural milieu and face each other in a way that may at times have to involve confrontation. Neither Paul nor our Lord Jesus shrank from confrontation when the time was right.

Some Suggestions

1. Consider multiculturalism positively, not negatively. It affirms the universality of the gospel, and the Christian community offers bridges of hope for reconciliation. It breaks down tribalism in the church. The New Testament affirms diversity within a unity. Cultural diversity is to be viewed as an enrichment.

2. Recognize the reality of cultural differences. Cultural relevance is not a negative. The importance of language, signs, symbols, historical traditions, value systems, and perceptions should be understood.

3. Learn to differentiate the important from the non-important, principle from practice. Is a tidy desk an automatic sign of integrity? Is efficiency as important as accountability?

4. Accept differences of expectations. Realize that our goals are based on perceptions, training, calling, and information input and are not necessarily identical to the goals of those who have a different background.

5. Be honest in appraising one's own missionary endeavor. In some parts of the world, mission has increasingly become high tech—using computers, faxes, professional managerial skills, and international currency transactions—while in other regions, mission is a matter of the simple preaching of the gospel. Be aware of the difficulties in linking the two together.

6. Give the whole picture when reporting back to one's constituency. Selective reporting can easily distort the reality of relationships. In all our publicity, when we begin new relationships, and in particular when requesting funds, it is important that we be honest and above board, giving all the relevant information and explaining it as necessary, including information about already existing relationships.

7. Take seriously John 17 in the face of the historic development of Christianity. How can the Holy Spirit, who is the refiner and transcender of culture, break down the denominational and confessional boundaries that often define and limit mission structures? We should not see evangelization from the basis of party spirit (1 Cor. 1:10ff). If we define and build relationships in terms of boundaries, we tend to erect confessional and denominational barriers which hinder greater Christian unity and relationships and therefore question the authenticity of the gospel.

Conclusion

Mission structures are related to the cultures that have given them birth. Their evolution has often taken on the form of the prevailing cultural norms and patterns. Of course, there have been rediscoveries of New Testament principles which have helped to shape contemporary structures, but these principles merely modify what has already come into existence through the culture of the time. Each age develops its own structural patterns as it rediscovers given truths from within the Scriptures and seeks to apply those truths within the prevailing contemporary situations.

Mission structures should be true to the original vision of their founders, and they need to recapture that vision again and again until the Lord gives a new vision. They also need to have the ability to change. The structures should be subservient to the vision and not the vision to the structures. Often there is a desire to change structures because we do not have the spiritual authority to change the vision.

The traditional sending cultures have normally operated by setting up an organization, with plans, goals, budgets, secretaries, equipment, etc., and then "doing mission" through that organization. The image of mission is that of an institution or organization. The impression is given that there was no mission before the colonial era which gave birth to the concept of institutional mission! This raises grave questions in the minds of some, particularly the historic churches of the East, which have for many centuries engaged in what they see as authentic mission, only to be told now that they were never missionary-minded.

The results are often twofold: either the national Christians do not attempt to engage in mission because they do not have the resources to set up and maintain institutions, or they set up a mission modeled on the traditional mission society and after some local fundraising they quickly transition to seeking support from wealthier countries all over the globe. The result is that traditional structures are replicated, and developing missions are stifled. Thankfully, there are also groups of national Christians that have gone ahead and engaged in mission without all the modern accoutrements.

How can a meaningful partnership be entered into, when on the one side mission is considered necessarily to involve an institution and on the other side it is seen as simply the gospel being proclaimed?

The biblical model is that of a witnessing community as the basis of mission. A witnessing community is organic—it gives birth to another witnessing community.

How can a Western mission body, having an institutional nature, enter into partnership agreements with an organic body, which by definition has no institutional characteristics, no chairman, no secretary, no board?

Will institutional mission structures be detrimental to the mission movements of Christ's church, particularly in restricted areas such as Muslim countries?

Paul was a Hellenized Jew. His roots were in Jewish culture, but he also understood Hellenic culture. Timothy was a

Judaized Greek. Culturally he was Greek, but as a God-fearer or proselyte he understood Judaism. Paul's method to reach the Gentiles was not to incarnate himself in the Gentile community, trying for decades to perfect his cross-cultural skills and be completely accepted by the Gentiles. Rather, he interfaced with Timothy, spent time teaching and training him, and then sent him to penetrate his own community. The result of Paul's ministry was that new congregations were planted that were self-sufficient, i.e., self-supporting, self-led, and self-propagating. These congregations could be termed witnessing communities, and they perpetuated themselves. They remained rooted in their culture, taking on its necessary forms and yet expressing the distinctiveness of the gospel through their new life. When syncretism occurred, correction was needed. When misunderstanding occurred, guidance was given. Hence Paul's letters directed to missionary situations.

While it is true that some traditional missionaries have exercised and continue to exercise eminently successful ministries in cross-cultural evangelism and church-planting, they are the exception. It needs to be recognized that the most effective work is done by the local community reproducing itself. The more common situation when a missionary tries to penetrate a community not his own is that he needs institutional support, with preparation, training, and encouragement as he faces culture shock, etc. Even with all these resources, he is not as successful as a member of the community itself.

How can a traditional sending missionary society enter into relationships with groups in other parts of the world to produce authentic witnessing communities that will replicate themselves?

Additional Questions

According to the Willowbank Report, the core of culture is the worldview; from this the value system emerges, which affects social behavior and institutions. How can we attain a biblical worldview from which value systems, social behavior structures, and institutions will develop?

Given that value systems are born out of worldviews, how can meaningful relationships develop between people who have different, but biblical, value systems? How can we separate the values that come from institutions, be they missionary or otherwise, from the prevailing culture and from the global culture?

Appendix: A Practical Example

The PIPKA Mission Board of the Muria Church of Java provides an excellent example in its basic principles of cooperation with the Mennonite Brethren Board of North America. They agreed on the following:

1. First and foremost, we acknowledge that we are members of the same family (Eph. 2:19). Hence, it is only natural for us to join hands and work together as equals.

2. Our "partnership" is not to be understood in terms of shareholders but is based on the concept of family members helping one another, of the parts of the body all being essential to the well-being of the whole. We need each other, and we need to help one another. The older and stronger is bound to help the weaker and younger.

3. There is room for diversity and differences, but these are not to be interpreted as disunity. Nor is there superiority or inferiority (1 Cor. 12:14-26).

4. Any kind of work in our partnership is to strengthen, build, and mature the local churches, so that in turn they are equipped to grow and multiply.

5. The program decisions are to be made on the field (i.e., the Mennonite Brethren Board and/or their representatives are to help implement and achieve PIPKA's goals and not their own).

6. Thus our equality is assured, since any "foreign" contributors are not holding an upper hand; neither are they larger shareholders.

7. Consequently, PIPKA is responsible for oversight and leadership:

a. PIPKA is to determine what personnel are to be recruited and accepted.

b. The partnership is subject to constant evaluation by all concerned.

c. PIPKA is responsible for running a missionary training program for candidates (be they Indonesian or foreigners).*

Patrick Sookhdeo was born of Muslim parents in Guyana, South America, and came to Christ while studying in Britain. Based in London, he is Director of In Contact Ministries, Director of the International Institute for the Study of Islam and Christianity, and Executive Secretary of Servants' Fellowship International. He pastors a multicultural inner-city congregation.

---

* Cristiano, C. (1982, October). PIPKA: An Indonesian response to mission. *International Bulletin, 6*(4).

6

A North American Response
to Patrick Sookhdeo

Paul McKaughan

I want to thank Patrick, as well as Bill Taylor, for giving me the opportunity to respond to Patrick's thoughtful paper. I respond not as a scholar, but rather as a practitioner, one who has been a missionary, missions manager, and hopefully a leader. We are people who are chosen or appointed to take people to places that they want to go. The destination may be intangible qualities such as peace, plenty, justice, or well-being, or they may be tangibles such as money, victory, a destination to be reached, or a city to be built. There is an unwritten contract between the follower and the leader to arrive at the ultimate destination that they have agreed upon. As such, results tend to be the main concern of leaders. These results could be both qualitative and/or quantitative. As we discuss partnership and missions and how culture relates to this process, my overriding concern is one of results.

Introduction

I have been involved in mission partnerships for some 30 years now. In the beginning, my partnerships were monocultural, in that I was a part of a very closely knit team of

Americans who committed themselves to a task and one another over a period of about 10 years. I have also been a part of the formation of 20 or 30 other monocultural teams around the world. During these years it has been my privilege to be involved in many bicultural or multicultural partnerships. I have worked as the minority American on a Brazilian consortium and in a Chinese group, both as a follower and as a leader. I have been a part of Anglo partnerships led by internationals. The outstanding fact is that in all of these relationships and partnerships I have been greatly enriched. I have gained a deeper understanding of myself and my own culture, and these experiences have given me a far greater appreciation for the diversity and strengths which exist in the international cultural diversity of Christ's body.

I would be remiss, however, if I did not state that for all of the personal benefit that I have gained (and some of these partnerships have been extremely productive), over the years there has grown within me a series of reservations flowing from the tremendous costs, both personal and financial, of maintaining both monocultural and multicultural partnerships. At times I have been dismayed by the paucity of results in light of the investment by all of the members of the group.

In today's economy, time equals money, and constantly we must ask ourselves how much time we can afford. Especially in international partnership, I find that the demands of time are exhausting. If real, honest, and open communications are to be carried on, to a large degree they must be done face to face and at great length. Communication through the "trade language" of English is a further complication. I must admit that many of the international partnerships that I have been a part of have been neither effective nor efficient and have resulted in solutions to problems that have been sub-optimal. Many times the results have been mere expressions of the lowest possible common denominator rather than a representation of the potential strengths that could be employed.

Even though my expectations over the years have become much more moderate and, I hope, more realistic, I remain convinced and convicted of the necessity of worldwide partnerships. This is not the result of some sanguine idealism, for the past 30 years' experience has tempered that. Rather, I remain convinced because of biblical truth—three truths, to be specific.

Three Biblical Foundations for Partnership

The first truth is that ministry always flows from relationship. My ministry flows from my relationship with God, through the person of Jesus Christ. In fact, my ministry flows from the relationship which existed in the Trinity that resulted in the creation of man and establishing mankind in relationship with one another. This communal relationship contains the discernible mirror image of the triune God. We give testimony to it as we work in concert. Failure to do so results in hindered prayers and impaired corporate effectiveness.

The second fact is that the Bible says that the demonstration of our oneness is the highest indication to a watching world that we love Him, our Christ, and that He loves us. If in fact this demonstration before a watching world is so important, then I must find mechanisms for making that visible. Partnership, both formal and informal, becomes a mandatory lifestyle. Pragmatically, partnerships in the world in which we live are not optional. They are not optional because every day we find that we are more interrelated. Technology as well as worldwide problems are binding us together as never before. The eternal, interrelated nature of the church, however, is more weighty than the existential reality of the age.

The biblical metaphors for the church as the body of Christ and the temple give me no alternative but to accept the fact that I was baptized into one body and Christ is the Head of that body. This is not a choice on my part, but rather the oneness of the body of Christ is sovereignly established and not optional. And if we are to give expression to that oneness, partnership relationships are essential.

There is one more important fact. There is a new wind of the Spirit of God which is drawing His body into all forms of visible and cooperative endeavors—partnerships. I know not

one of our elder statesmen in the international missions
community who would not say that the degree of cooperation
and partnership that we are seeing today is unparalleled in his
or her experience. This is not because we are better people or
that the need is greater. This is the drawing of the Holy Spirit
and His application of biblical truth to our generation.

Productive Christian Partnerships Are Not Natural

Now for a point of realism. Good, productive partnerships
are not natural. In fact, usually partnership is just one more
way for me to get my own way. Partnerships are usually a
means for me to acquire your financial or technical resources
if I need them. Partnerships can be the way for me to enroll
laborers to carry out my ends at a cheaper cost. In the past,
my agenda has controlled the desirability for partnership. (I
use a generic human "I" and "my" because we are affected by
the fall.) This is natural because our own egotistical desire is
many times a significant part of the driving force behind our
ministry. We clothe it in biblical language, but nonetheless,
self-expression, self-actualization, and egotism are often operational norms in Christian ministries. The song "My Way,"
by North American entertainer Frank Sinatra, is not just the
theme of the West—it is the theme of the fallen human heart.
Satan will use anything to keep us from working together.

In commerce you can build partnership on the basis of
profit, return on invested capital (ROIC), etc. Having a com-
mercially accepted absolute like this makes working together
easier, because differences can be resolved by mathematical
means, profit or loss. This type of "bottom line" partnership
may be sufficient for the business world, where profit can be
the arbiter. But in the world in which you and I live, the world
in which we are seeking to carry out the biblical mandate,
much confusion exists over the "bottom line"—proclamation
versus holism, church planting over and against nurture, print
media or electronics. All vie for our attention, and to those who
are involved they seem to be the most effective approaches. *My*
"bottom line" keeps me from *our* "bottom line."

Pride a Basic Deterrent to Partnership

In many of our partnerships, we find it very difficult to have confidence that all involved are under the same Lord and Head of the body that we are, and I have the suspicion that I hear God's voice much more clearly than you do. Somehow, my motives are more pure and my interpretation of His Word is the right one. When there is the power of either men, finances, or technology on my side and I have the advantage, I become more adamant in my representation of my divine truth and calling. Many times I do so by making my culture, my way of doing things, dominant in our partnership.

Often this can happen purely through the exercise of our communication. In international cooperation and partnerships we tend to function through the trade language of English. While this facilitates our communication at a factual level, it often blurs and inhibits our communication at the level of heart and feelings. It tends to shroud real meaning with an aura of communication. My facility with English can enable me to dominate the process and sound more spiritual, profound, or astute. To overcome this barrier takes a great commitment of time as well as emotional and spiritual capital. Above all, it takes selfless humility.

Biblical Culture and Acceptance of Diversity

Culture is very important to who we are. Many times the dominant party in an international partnership even clothes his or her culture with the mantle of "Christian." There is no truly "Christian culture" this side of heaven. There is no "biblical culture" this side of eternity. Although God's revelation in Jesus Christ was culture specific, in that Jesus grew up and was raised within a Middle Eastern culture of His day, that culture is not normative for us today. Yet the divine revelation of Jesus Christ in that specific culture provides for us all that we require for faith and godliness, including knowledge about relationships with one another.

But we must be careful. If I have the ability to define what is biblical for you, this can become another type of ideological and cultural imperialism. There is a tremendous danger when I make my cultural interpretation of Scripture normative. It is dangerous to judge my interpretation as right over and against yours. Sin fragmented and poisoned man's relationships to one another, as well as his relationship to his Creator. Redemption begins the process of bringing us together, but that is a long process. It starts from the position of alienation, which often results in my saying, "My culture is the only right way," since sin usually exalts self.

We all truly need to discover our identities as children of the King. We must not eliminate cultural differences, but rather we must raise them to the fore so the assumptions can be examined and so honest, divergent conclusions about biblical facts can enrich our understanding of divine truth. It is in that diversity of the body of Christ that we have its unique giftedness. Through that diversity we increase our under-standing of divine revelation. Only when we experience the multicultural composite before the throne of God will we fully understand the picture of God's revelation.

If we are to form meaningful partnerships, it is incumbent upon both parties entering into the relationship to recognize their unique contribution. Each culture endows those who are raised within it with certain distinct characteristics that be-come a part of the organization's or individual's personality, a way of coping with the environment, social or physical. It is true that there are basic needs and desires to which we all respond; however, we respond in very distinct ways to those stimuli. Christians always seem to have two significant—and at times, opposing—reactions to environmental stimuli. At one end of the continuum is a possessive holding on and defending of my uniqueness. At times, even more than just defending, I am involved in a battle to make my uniqueness normative for all people with whom I interact.

At the other end of the continuum is a denial of these characteristics. We can sublimate these unique ways of inter-facing with reality under a "permission" which we baptize with the name of "Christian culture." We appeal to the truths of the Scripture which state that in Christ there is neither bond nor free, Jew nor Gentile, male nor female. We extend this fact and argument to say that for the Christian, there should be no cultural uniqueness. There is only Christ, who should unite us. This, however, is to ignore who we are as people. This violates the truth. We do see things differently. We perceive even physical phenomena in distinct ways. This is part of our divine corporate and individual giftedness, not a mere result of our sinful natures.

It seems as though integration comes as the cross of Christ cuts across my self-centered distinctiveness, as I surrender my right of defense and my imperial aspirations to Christ and His kingdom. As a Christian, I must die to my way of doing things. To me, what the Apostle Paul is saying is that I as a Christian must cherish your uniqueness. This takes supernatural, divine grace. I must recognize my own patterns, but I must put you first as a brother or sister. Was this not what the incarnation was all about? The Word became flesh and dwelt among man in a particular time and in a particular race and culture. Ultimately, He even surrendered His life according to the dictates of that culture. In the resurrection, we have not some androgynous expression of uniform life, but rather a supernatural manifestation of oneness in diversity as we extend the kingdom community together. In any successful international partnership, our cultures must be carried to the cross of Jesus Christ. And just as Christ died in my place, so must I allow my culture, my way of doing things, to be crucified with Christ. As I die to self so must I die to my culture. It is a part of me. Culture is not in any way totally bad. But it has been affected by the fall, and therefore it must be redeemed. International partnerships may well be a part of this redemptive process, because they force all of us to examine our culture, our way of doing things, in a new light. I am amazed at the degree of cultural superiority that we all carry with us insidiously, subconsciously, pervasively confirming our own superiority. In this way we re-erect or hold to the walls of partition which Christ has broken down.

All of the words that we use and hold dear and think we understand—words like loyalty, fellowship, and leadership—are words that carry incredible cultural baggage. We know we should be loyal. We know we should have fellowship. We know that leadership should exist. However, the stresses come in with the exercise of these basic principles. It is not the what but the how. And within the exercise of the how is where we collide, often with devastating results, with the phenomenon of the "unmet expectation."

Unmet Expectations

Perhaps the greatest obstacle to successful partnerships that I have encountered has been in this area of expectation. A wise man once told me that we did not have "personality conflicts," we had conflicts of "unmet expectations." That is, I in my dealings with you have a set of rules by which I expect that we will interact with one another. I may never have articulated these rules to you, but somehow these rules are the behaviors of "good people," real "mature Christian leaders" in my estimation, and when you do not act according to my set of rules or expectations, then immediately we enter into conflict, because you have not measured up to the internal regime which I have been given by my culture. In international partnership, these agendas or expectations are rarely articulated by either partner in a proposed partnership. And when our expectations are not met, then there is a tremendous sense of betrayal that surfaces, often accompanied by bitterness. This is one of the principal ways we express our ethnocentrism and self-centeredness. It is incumbent upon all of us if we are to work in meaningful international partnerships first of all to recognize our own expectations, and secondly, to learn to verbalize them in such a way that will enable us to harmonize our differences and create common expectations.

All vestiges of God's image in an individual and his or her culture are incomplete. Together we approach greater completeness. We need all of our cultural diversity and giftedness to begin to approach that visible manifestation of what the body of Christ is and can be in the world of fallen mankind. There are biblical norms of relationship that we always must strive for. One of those norms is the acceptance of brothers and sisters as they are. We are one in Christ, the Scripture says. The work of the cross of Jesus Christ broke down the barriers between man and woman, bondman and free, Greek and barbarian. This does not mean that in order for partnerships to take place, there must be some sort of homogeneous, universal culture free from the distinctiveness that sets apart various cultures. It is significant that before the throne of God, at the culmination of the story of redemption, there will be men and women of every tribe, tongue, and nation, and they will all, in their various diverse manners, worship the Lamb that was slain. So in partnership we do not strive for a homogenized "Christian" culture, but rather we strive to allow the Holy Spirit to express Himself through the diversity of our cultures, through the strengths and giftedness of our various cultural expressions. We do this through walking together by faith, accepting one another as we have been accepted by the Father. Christ's call to the people of God is universal for all who are members of His body. He calls us as He has gifted us. He calls us for specific as well as universal commission. Diversity, not conformity, is our strength. Christ is both a "tribal God" and a "universal God." It is not either/or. We are part of a people where there is no male or female, bond or free, Greek or barbarian. We are also uniquely gifted individually and corporately in and by our cultures.

You and I are responsible for our reactions and our relationships, first of all to God and secondly to our fellow brothers in Christ. The Scripture teaches us that if my relationship to you is not in good order, there is no point for me to go to God's altar with a sacrifice. If my relationship with my wife is not in good repair, my prayers are going to be hindered, says the Scripture. Therefore, I must always place the responsibility squarely on my own shoulders in this partnership quest. I find great comfort in the fact that God always accepts me where I am, He accepts me as I am, He accepts me with my monocultural biases, He accepts me with my prejudice. As I acknowledge my biases and repent of my superior attitudes, He takes me where He ultimately wants me to go in terms of my broader acceptance of brothers and sisters. I am responsible to allow Christ to be formed in me and work out the partnership model that He has in His mind for the church. To do less is to be egotistical and sinfully self-centered. Repentance must always be a mark of our reintegration through Christ's redemptive work. We have all fallen short, and the emphasis must be on the personal and corporate recognition of our fallenness and our falling short of the standard of God as set in Scripture. We have all fallen short even of our own standards in these various areas, and that is first where we need to repent. From there we can go on to examine together what partnership means in the light of the Word and all our insights into it.

Mutual Benefits

Partnerships are always based on perceived mutual benefits to both parties. Many times the benefits may not be the same for all participants in a partnership; however, it is extremely important that all elements hoping and seeking to enter into partnership know what they bring to the endeavor and what they expect to take from it. All need a realistic appraisal of their assets, their liabilities, and their needs. This appraisal needs to be done from my perspective, and then I need to look at the issue from the perspective of my future partner. Forced alliances do not last very long.

Least Complicated Partnership

The least complicated model of partnership that I have been able to observe is the one where there is a dominant partner, the partner who sets the cultural agenda or styles for the partnership. The cultural norms are more readily determined, and adaptation by the second party is more natural in such an arrangement. It is true that in this type of partnership the dominant partner can become abusive or exploitative. But the junior or senior partner can and must withdraw if ultimate biblical values are threatened. There should never be a stubborn insistence upon "my way," no matter how it is cloaked in spiritual terms.

Fight or Flight

Partnership internationally will not be easy. It is contrary to our nature. Conflict is not something that we look forward to, and the "fight or flight syndrome" is often evidenced in international partnership. On the one hand, we either "fight" for our own way of doing things, or we take "flight," run and ignore our differences. We sublimate them to the point where they are pushed below the surface of our minds but fester until they explode to the surface. Partnerships take immense time, and the question is still open as to whether we can afford the amount of time necessary to form meaningful partnerships internationally on a deep and personal level, or whether our partnerships will be structured on a merely utilitarian, businesslike basis.

Pre-Partnership Requirements

Here are some pre-partnership requirements if we are going to be able to build upon our cultural strengths rather than stumble over our weaknesses.

First of all, we must know what our dominant cultural values are. There are tools today for us to do that. A compact and helpful book by anthropologists Sherwood Lingenfelter and Marvin Mayers entitled *Ministering Cross-Culturally* groups a multitude of cultures on 12 axes as pictured on the following page.*

---

* Lingenfelter, S., & Mayers, M. (1986). *Ministering cross-culturally.* Grand Rapids: Baker Book House.

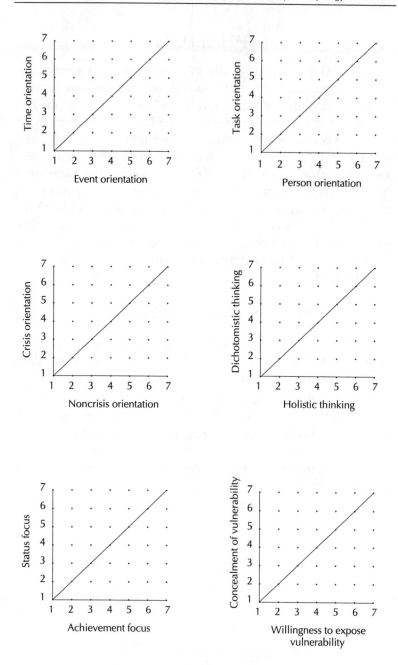

A Model of Basic Values

Simple tools like these can begin to help us as we communicate with one another and seek to understand one another. But our understanding of others is predicated upon an appreciation and understanding of ourselves, where we feel superior and why we feel superior.

Secondly, it is important to know what we want out of a partnership. We must be honest about this. If we want cheaper manpower to carry out our program, we must say so. Or if we are seeking financial resources or access to certain technologies which we deem necessary for the furthering of the cause of Christ in our own nation or in other parts of the world, we must clearly articulate the reason that we are seeking to enter into an international partnership.

Thirdly, we must be clear about our organizational or cultural limitations. I have a very good friend working in the United States among the African-American community, trying to establish a mission movement. If it were perceived that this movement is influenced unduly by the Anglo community in the United States, my friend could never achieve his goal. Therefore, any cooperation and partnership into which he enters must allow him the visibility and the independence to truly say, "This is ours as an African-American community." There are limits placed upon mission organizations in North America both by governments and by donor constituencies that demand a degree of fiscal accountability that may not be acceptable to potential international partners, but for Americans these areas are non-negotiable. There may be some flexibility in the satisfaction of the minimum requirements. There may be stylistic or cultural issues over which we have little control. They are the givens at this point in time. It is absolutely essential that we know what the limitations are. These must be treated honestly and not as mere negotiating ploys to further our own ends.

Five Areas Which Require Agreement

There are a number of areas over which there must be agreement if meaningful cross-cultural partnerships are to be effective. Here are five primary areas or elements of an effective partnership. In each one of these areas, there exist cultural expectations which must be clarified so as to avoid unnecessary conflict in the partnership.

1. Appropriate Leadership

The first element of an effective partnership is appropriate leadership. What are the expectations for the leader in the partnership? Will there be a leader? Will this leader be expected just to moderate, or will he be expected to act as a military commander, sending people out to fight and perhaps die? The role of the leader in a partnership is extremely important, and not only the role but also the style—how that leader will carry out his or her responsibilities. Is the leader to be a consensus builder, to keep everyone happy and not ruffle feathers? Is the leader to be stylistically a manager, with orderly processes above everything else, or is he or she to be a visionary entrepreneur who leads by force of personality and vision? I have seen two international partnerships self-destruct because of expectations of leadership that were not realistic or assumptions that were made as to the style and expectations for the leader, none of which were ever articulated either by the leader coming in or by the organization that was to be led. The situation ultimately led to the dissolution of the partnerships.

2. Purpose of the Partnership

There must be a clear understanding by everyone involved in the partnership as to the purpose of this partnership. Why is this partnership or group being formed? Can every member of the partnership paint a word picture of the purpose in his or her own words? Is the purpose clear to all? Do they understand the purpose, and is it compelling? Will all of the members of the partnership truly sacrifice to achieve the purpose? When dealing with purpose, we must deal with the issue of hidden agendas as well. Hidden agendas within a partnership in the body of Christ become the sores that fester and ultimately rob the partnership of vitality and breed distrust and suspicion.

3. Agreed-Upon Processes

In any partnership there must be agreed-upon processes. That is, how in this partnership do we make decisions? Do we discuss all matters among the participants and arrive at a consensus? Do we vote and go by majority rule? How do we resolve conflicts? Do we follow merely democratic process, or do we stay in protracted prayer and interaction until a consensus is reached on a conflict? How do we deal with successional leadership? How do we modify our original purposes in the light of changing circumstances? For a healthy partnership, it is important that our cultural expectations in terms of processes be clearly understood. We can thus avoid a great deal of misunderstanding.

4. Division of Labor

We need to consider division of labor, meaning who in the partnership does what. This is where accountability becomes real. In a partnership, not everyone can do everything that they would like to do. Not every member can lead all the time. It is extremely important that all within the partnership know the responsibilities which they are assuming. If it is funding, how will those funds be released and on what timetable? For a North American mission, this question is problematic, because almost always the funds are available only as raised, and one never knows exactly how a constituency is going to respond to a funding request. This must be clearly understood by all parts of a partnership. The responsibility and the division of labor must be clearly understood and assumed by all of the various partners.

5. Relational Style

The final item has to do with relationship and communication—the climate in which the partnership will function. It has to do with an appropriate relational style. Is that style going to be formal, where all members of the partnership come and meet together in their dark business suits and use Roberts' Rules of Order? Or will it be informal, where everyone functions together on the basis of an informal, free give and take and meets in casual wear? Will relationships be intimate and close or distant and formal? In personal confrontation, what is appropriate, and what is out of bounds? What will be the norms of good sense and godly conduct that will govern our relationships one to the other? Have we aligned our expectations?

These are, to my mind, the big five over which the partners must have agreement as much as possible. The right or wrong answers to these five components are culturally conditioned. In an international partnership, the partners must agree on the cultural norm they will adopt in each case. I have seen partnerships destroyed because of the perception on the part of leaders that they were treated in an inappropriate fashion, in an undignified or even disrespectful manner. All actions were performed unknowingly and were quite unintentional. The communications process is in itself extremely difficult, when the expectations are that the other person must know, understand, and play by my cultural rules, and I need not articulate those rules for him or her. The very articulation sometimes is a painful process of exposing oneself, but it cannot be avoided.

The Problem and Pain of Partnership

All of us engaged in this partnership quest tend to be overworked. Even more than overworked, in the Christian world we tend to be underfinanced and understaffed. We are also often overstressed by the competing demands placed on us. Lack of adequate time is one of the greatest stressors. Because of this, we must consciously ask ourselves what is a realistic expectation in the way of partnerships internationally and cross-culturally, before we increase our load of stress, time, and work. How much additional time and emotional investment can I give to these efforts? Here, I believe, are three strategies that can be employed by the mission executive to deal with this problem. Two strategies have to do with the person's own organizational operations. The third has to do with the mission system.

Top-Down

The first strategy for partnership concerns the unique function of the chief executive or leader, and most of us here are chief executives. One of the primary functions of the chief executive is to be a living symbol of the organizational culture or values. In that symbolism it is important that partnership be raised as one of the primary values of the corporate life of the mission or church. Symbolic actions of partnership are very powerful, especially when they are implemented at the operational grassroots level by empowered people. These two strategies go together—top-down symbolism and bottom-up operational partnership agreements. The leader must personify the quest for partnership as he or she relates to others outside the organization.

Bottom-Up

The second strategy involves the area of decision making. As leaders, too often we centralize our decision-making process. In the world of today, we must empower others to make decisions. That is, we must push decision making down through the various levels of our organization to the most basic operational level where people function and work towards world evangelization. One of the solutions to the partnership stress issue is to force decision making and thus the responsibility for the formation of partnerships to the operational level, rather than trying to deal with all of the issues and concepts at the highest administrative levels. If the partnership was built at the operational level, then problem solving can be done at that same level. A management consultant once said, "In today's environment, you must give up control to control or influence the really important things." To do this success-fully, the operational people must know that partnership is the way "our organization wants to go," and they must have a clear understanding as to the limits and parameters within which they can form alliances and agreements to partner.

Honest Partnership Brokers

There is one other technique that I believe must be explored with far greater passion within the Christian organizational community. Phill Butler has mentioned it. I would highlight it. The creation of partnership brokers within our international communities is an urgent necessity. Though I as an opera-tional executive cannot handle the time demands or the stress of a lot of partnerships, people who sense a unique calling from God to create partnerships can deal with the emotional and time demands of nurturing such partnerships. They can also create a specialized body of knowledge which will enable them to be used of God to pull these alliances and partnerships together more effectively. Up until now, the major demands in partnerships have been made on people who are operationally extended beyond what is reasonable to expect. We are only now beginning to see individuals and organizations emerge within our missions community that sense as their unique calling from God the formation of partnerships and strategic alliances. They can be the honest brokers who facilitate many of the partnerships for the future. This is especially true when talking about the vertical integration of a large number of ministry forces and expertise. It takes someone uniquely gifted and called to facilitate such a partnership. The long-term viability of these consultants and facilitators will be determined by their willingness to be servants of the various ministries, rather than manipulating the ministries to fulfill the ends of the facilitator.

Personal Reflections

The first partnership upon which I embarked in Brazil was a personal failure. It was a disaster because our expectations with regards to the five things that I have just mentioned were never clarified, and yet we made judgments concerning one another that undermined our relationships. We applied moral content to those behaviors, judging one another spiritual or unspiritual. This ultimately destroyed our ability to work together.

The second partnership, which I went into with a greater degree of realism, was a partnership in the beginning just to accomplish certain professional goals, productivity goals. It was very much like a business partnership. As we worked together to achieve those goals of productivity, we learned much more about one another and increased the areas of mutual commitment to the point where there were few distinguishing marks between us: we almost became one. We built on our first tottering steps of successes, and in so doing, our knowledge about ourselves increased and our reactions to one another and our knowledge of the elements involved in the partnership grew, and it became a very fulfilling and productive collaboration.

I would like to make an important observation about partnerships, either international or domestic. I have observed both personally and in my organizational life that when I am forced to fight for my rights, I am usually wrong. It seems as though the biblical norm is that I am always to humble myself, and in due time, He will exalt me if that is His will. I often find that when I am forced to fight for my rights, then my ego is too much involved in this partnership issue, and I must deal with my own motivations. Even in partnership I must remember both parties are under the ultimate control of the Head of the church.

The Potential of Partnerships

As I have observed mission strategy over the last 30 years, I have seen us, the missions community, time and again become enamored with a particular operational strategy or way of looking at the world. This way of looking at the world or that strategy has been elevated in such a way as to present it as the answer to the problem of world evangelization. Whether it is unreached peoples, church growth, partnership, signs and wonders, theological education by extension, or other good and worthy emphases, we must recognize that down through history, the greatest advances of Christ's kingdom have come because of sovereign acts of God's grace, where we as missions, with all of our strategy and all of our giftedness, have, in effect, almost been bystanders. It is important that we interject into the discussion of partnership a note of reality recognizing that it is not partnership which will bring about the evangelization of the world and the discipling of the nations, but rather it is a sovereign act of God's grace that will bring these things about. Partnership may be a major contributor to the process, however, and we should follow this course, because it is biblical and because God in His sovereignty seems to be applying this biblical truth to our generation today in a unique way. Partnership will save no one individual or guarantee the discipling of a single nation. It is a path of obedience to God to accomplish His ends. We don't create the winds of God's Spirit; we only read them. We could form all kinds of partnerships, vertically and horizontally integrated, and still have little more than complex structures costing ever-increasing amounts of money. The most effective utilization of partnerships will be when we respond unitedly to specific actions of God's Spirit. As He blesses these unions, we will see greater effectiveness and efficiency as the body functions in the manner for which it was designed.

The last thing I would mention in terms of cross-cultural partnerships is that there is no substitute for spending time together in the presence of the Head of the church. This is absolute priority, and there is no higher. We must spend time in His Word, allowing Him to speak to us both individually and collectively. We must spend time in prayer, listening to brothers' and sisters' hearts as they cry out to God for their own lives and for our work together. We must listen to His voice through brothers and sisters who are perceiving Him through another cultural filter, which I need in order to be more complete in Christ.

Multicultural partnerships are difficult. They are extremely time consuming, and often their productivity, in my experience, has been sub-optimal. However, if in fact we are a people of the Book, we must go back to the biblical imperatives, and those imperatives say that we are one in Christ and that we must in fact act that way under the direction of the Holy Spirit. As a coordinated body, we must do His will and His purposes in time and in space. We do these things through the blending of our cultural strengths and talents. This is the essence of cross-cultural partnership.

A North American, Paul McKaughan served from 1962 to 1975 in Brazil, first with Bethany Fellowship and then with OC International as coordinator of planning. He has also taught at the Word of Life and Free Methodist seminaries in São Paulo, Brazil. In 1975 he and his family returned to the USA to work with OC. He subsequently served as Chief Executive Officer of Mission to the World, the foreign missions arm of the Presbyterian Church in America. From 1987 to 1989, Mr. McKaughan worked with the Lausanne Committee on World Evangelization, until his appointment as Executive Director of EFMA in the USA. He and his wife, Joanne, have three grown children born in Brazil. He is a member of the WEF Missions Commission.

7

A Nigerian Response
to Patrick Sookhdeo

Maikudi Kure

Rev. Dr. Patrick Sookhdeo worked very hard on his paper. All the facts he mentioned are there. We must appreciate his efforts in bringing us back to biblical facts about partnership.

We thank the Lord for the support in different forms from the Western world to the non-Western. Many churches and related church organizations have been developed, and many more are coming up. Most of them are depending on Western support. That is how it has been going on for many years up to this date.

In this era, many seminars, workshops, and conferences are being conducted on the subject of partnership in mission between the Western and non-Western world, but we are not making progress as we should, because of some issues mentioned in Dr. Sookhdeo's paper.

The main issue to be tackled is that big obstacle that is disturbing the progress of partnership between these two parties: financial paternalism. In the beginning, everything was done by the missionaries from the Western world. The nationals (non-Western) were babies and were financially poor, but they were very rich in culture.

The church now is mature. The nationals took up the leadership. Many projects were introduced. Some are completed, some are in progress, and many have been abandoned because the Western missionaries who initiated the project have gone, and funds stopped coming. Many times the nationals look to the parents (the Western world) to supply and to provide funds and materials for these projects, even for staff salaries. The money and materials may continue to come, but they may be accompanied by a parental directive on how to use the funds and the materials. This system has been going on for many years, and the Westerners never learned from the previous occurrences. The paternalism in different forms is conducted in the style of, "He who pays the piper calls for the tune!"

The language of today is "partnership in mission works." All parties are trying to bring solution to the previous problems, but they are avoiding the roots of those problems, which are present on both the Western and non-Western sides.

The best solution to these problems is to see the need for change in the whole system of give and take between the two sides. The fact that we must face is culture, the cultures of non-Western leadership transplanted into Western church leadership. Sincerity and trust are at the root of accountability. Many documents have been prepared and signed as an agreement for partnership, but we are not willing or ready to face the cultural differences.

- We must be sincere.
- We must trust each other.
- Let the partnership be without paternalism.
- Let the Spirit of give and take lead.
- Respect each other's cultures.

Maikudi Kure, a Nigerian, has served through the Evangelical Church of West Africa (ECWA), Jos, Nigeria, in various capacities: pastor, principal of Bible school, Bible translator (English to Hausa, his mother tongue), and director of a mission organization (EMS of ECWA). Currently he is Manager of Literature and Publication of ECWA Productions Limited (EPL). He and his wife have six children.

8

A Latin American Response to Patrick Sookhdeo

Federico Bertuzzi

I am thankful to Patrick for the excellent work he has presented, and I wish to add some of my own thoughts in order to enrich his valuable paper regarding cultural issues that affect international cooperation.

The Old Global Schemes No Longer Work

I agree, as Patrick has stated, that today we cannot simply continue functioning with the scheme, still in use today, of dividing humanity between First World, Second, and Third; nor can we accept the concept of the Developed World and the Developing World. With the dissolution of the communist bloc, which we have only recently observed, and the end of the Cold War, which had marked us since the Second World War, the old geopolitical world mindset simply cannot continue. To this reality we must add the fact of the revolution in communications media—whether the revolution which comes when we travel by jets to any corner of the globe within hours, or the empire of novel and instantaneous communications through fax electronics or electronic mail by satellite, to mention only a few. Yes, our world has changed, and this is obvious! And these changes affect relationships between Christians of all geographical locations.

If we are dealing with the theme, "Towards Interdependent Partnerships," I understand that we do it with the ultimate purpose of clarifying some issues in the mutual relationships which have felt the impact of misunderstandings, or for the purpose of removing roadblocks which we have not thus far been able to eliminate, to the extent that we can take full advantage of the potential which each of us has for the benefit of the extension of the kingdom of God. And it is our desire that these days which we spend in Manila will lead us to take the measures which will concretely help accelerate completion of the remaining task of world evangelization.

Evaluative Criteria and Measurement of Results

There are different ways to evaluate culture, as Patrick has well stated early in his paper. There are different expectations related to the desired results, as well as in the methods or the objectives which allow final evaluation of outcomes. For some, statistics dictate the sentence of approval or disapproval; others give little value to numbers, and they tend to reject the practice of evaluating matters coldly, governed by simple numbers.

I remember some time ago having read an article by Alvin Toffler in which he projected tomorrow's world as he saw it. We can see this world emerging today. Toffler argued that the future clear demarcation of peoples would not be on the basis of the "haves" and the "have nots," as is done today, but rather on whether countries are rapid or slow. That is to say, whether the response medium of a particular society is rapid and agile, or whether the society will require a natural and slow process of change. The response rate is due in part to the influence of technology, but other factors also play a role.

It is clear to me that in Anglo Saxon countries, due to a variety of reasons (discipline, specialization, task division, better time administration, economic solvency, greater number of personnel, etc.), decision making, communication of adopted measures, and the implementation of such measures are surprisingly more agile, direct, and pragmatic than in the majority of our countries of the "South."

Among us of the "South" this process takes place more as we come and go, seeking to reach consensus, seeking broad-based support or trying to avoid hurt feelings. The process of decision making is considerably slower (unless we are dealing with organizations managed by strongman personalities). And for us, once we have made the decision, even to the point of implementation, there are also long delays, due among other reasons to the lack of specialized personnel. What's more, the few people who might be available with convictions or capacities for the task have their hands tied up in a thousand other duties. It is not unusual to find Christian workers who, simply to subsist, must carry out two or three Christian ministries at the same time, earning in that manner what is needed to sustain their families. Obviously, they are unable to dedicate the time necessary to achieve excellent results in any of their jobs. It is common to listen to the pain of these servants who never meet the demands of their jobs.

When we speak of international partnership, we cannot but keep these two factors in mind. On the one hand, for some it would appear as if they (from the "South") are being bowled over by those of the other culture (from the "North") with their demands, deadlines, and accountability reports; on the other hand, we are seen as too slow, irresponsible regarding our given word, and untrustworthy for future projects. Dealing with this situation requires a good dose of maturity and mutual understanding. If we wish to advance into an interdependent partnership characterized by maturity and efficiency, we must understand, accept, and react to one another within this realistic framework which offers its own logical limitations. The issue is not so much changing the mentality and paradigm of one another, but rather understanding how to function within this reality.

The Barrier Imposed by Language

I want to add something not stated in Patrick's paper, but which I feel is a factor worthy of consideration and which slips by ignored in certain circles.

There is no doubt that English is the international language of excellence. It is the commercial, technological, and diplomatic language, and it is assumed, of course, that it is the missiological language as well. But is it really? In international evangelical forums, it is the expected language. Given the influence of Great Britain throughout the late centuries of colonization which it carried out in North America and the countries of Africa, Asia, and the South Pacific, obviously the English language became rooted, if not as the dominant language, at least as a second language. But this was not what happened in the extensive continent of Central and South America, where Spanish and Portuguese were the languages imposed by the conquering forces of the Iberian peninsula. This has led to the situation that, while English is considered an important language to know, in reality there are not many who speak it well. Only a very small percentage of the privileged ones who have had opportunity to live for years in or emigrate to North America can today speak English fluently.

Christian leaders who are good representatives of the 50 million Latin American evangelicals have told me repeatedly that either they are not taken into account because they do not speak English, or they have self-eliminated themselves from international meetings because of this very real situation. It is a "fashion" that in these international events, English has always been the only possible means of communication offered. In some cases, simultaneous translation is utilized, but always, the person who has to depend on this alternative does not feel fully integrated into the general spirit of the event. I assume that even beyond Latin America, similar situations take place which affect the fluidity of international contact.

The Delicate Subject
of Financial Cooperation

This is one of the most delicate aspects of partnership and a most difficult one to deal with. Working from the diverse cultural reality which Patrick has already developed, I believe that we have advanced in the mutual efforts to discover viable and more practical ways of facing the issue. Nevertheless, I want to present my thoughts, the fruit of constant observation and personal experience, regarding some of the latent points that must be taken into account.

We have, on the one hand, the donor who understands that he is responsible for the financial gift (whether because in his country the laws are very restrictive, or the original donors require it), and therefore he exerts meticulous control over how, in what ways, and for what the financial gift can be used. This situation leads inevitably to a directive attitude which, as we know, can interfere with and seriously disturb the task in a context where cultures react differently from the donor's culture.

On the other hand, the recipient of the gift can react in two different ways (particularly if these matters have not been previously and conveniently sorted out). Either the recipient will develop a total submission to the wishes of the donor because he simply does not wish to lose the funds, or he will begin to develop the sour taste of submission which he neither desires nor feels he should accede to. Either of these options inevitably creates, sooner or later, one of the greater stumbling blocks to international partnership.

This matter I mention here only in an abbreviated form, but I consider that it merits a more profound and detailed treatment if we are going to grow into a partnership that is mature and effective and that fulfills its true objectives.

International Partnership
in Latin America

As I go deeper into the kinds of partnership that take place in the context which I know best, Latin America, I wish to offer as an example the growing partnership in the world of foreign missions. The fact is that this is a new and growing phenomenon in most cases in our Iberoamerican continent. In our continent we have the president of an international missionary association, Pastor Rudy Girón of Guatemala, who represents the growing missionary movement which has taken root in Latin America. In the diverse 20 nations across our America, this movement takes on different characteristics according to the diverse continental regions.

In my country, Argentina, the movement is called "World Missions"; in Paraguay, it is called CONAMI (National Missions Committee); in Brazil, it is COMIBAM-Brazil; in Venezuela, it is CNM (National Missionary Committee); in Costa Rica, it is FEDEMEC (Missionary Federation of Costa Rica); in Guatemala, it is CONEMM (National Evangelical Mission to the World Commission). And this is but a partial list of the composite. We feel we are members of a brotherhood in COMIBAM (Cooperation of Iberoamerican Missions). At the same time, we serve as the missions commission of CONELA (Confraternity of Evangelicals of Latin America), which represents World Evangelical Fellowship in the continent. Therefore, we are learning the difficult art of international relationships and can already see the progress which is being made in this learning process. Thanks to the Lord, we are relating not only as Latins, but also as Latins with Anglos, Africans, and Asians, and we desire that these interrelationships will grow on a continuing basis.

A Continental Plan
to Reach the Unreached

In October, 1992, in San Jose, Costa Rica, we will hold for the first time in our Latin American continent the Adopt-A-People Consultation. We are inviting three key people from each country of our continent as well as the two Iberian lands.

One of the three is to be a leader of the national evangelical alliance, one will be a representative of the national missionary movement, and one will be a research and computer expert. The goal is to have between 70 and 80 people who represent the primary evangelical ecclesiastical and missionary streams of the continent. Together we want to analyze, debate, dream, pray for, and develop a strategy in order to involve and commit more than 50 million evangelicals of the continent to reach some 3,000 UNREACHED people groups—this represents 25 percent of the total people group task.

We ask you to pray for this meeting, which we expect will be historic, where we also will strategize the most practical way to mobilize our continent towards its global missionary job. Above all, we want prayer support, as well as finances to cover the flights of some of the brothers who have the greatest need.

Concrete Actions on Behalf of the Lost

It is my desire, as that of all of us present in Manila, that we will leave here not only better informed about the value of partnerships, but also with some concrete things that will demonstrate in a credible and practical manner our Lord's commandments about what it means to be one body.

Federico A. Bertuzzi, an Argentine, is the founder and national director of Misiones Mundiales in his country. He is also Vice President of COMIBAM International, Latin American Director of PM International, and director of the COMIBAM publications department. He is married with three children.

9

Control in Church/Missions Relationship and Partnership

Jun Vencer

About 2,000 years ago, Jesus Christ commanded His disciples, "'Go and make disciples of the nations...'" (Matt. 28:19). Given the realities of that time, the Great Commission was "mission impossible." It was:

• Physically impossible because there were no planes, cars, telephones, faxes, radios, or televisions.

• Numerically impossible because there were only about 500 disciples.

• Financially impossible because the total asset of the church was estimated at only $10,000.

• Sociologically impossible because most of the early converts came from among the poor and outcasts and were not held in high esteem.

• Legally impossible because preaching the gospel was considered a crime.

And yet the early disciples "turned the world upside down" (Acts 17:6). To them, lack of adequate material resources was not a hindrance. When God's people obeyed, God gave a mighty harvest. Today about 1.7 billion people profess Christ as

Savior. The ratio of Christians to non-Christians is narrowing. D. L. Moody once said, "It can be done, it must be done." The task of world evangelization is fulfillable. As Habakkuk puts it, "The earth will be filled with the knowledge of God as the waters cover the sea" (Hab. 2:14). Every second brings that future closer to us when "'this gospel of the kingdom shall be preached to all peoples, and then the end shall come'" (Matt. 24:14).

But whose task is missions? It is not the task of missionaries only. Not all Christians are called as missionaries. Neither is it the task simply of Western missions or of Third World missions (with the demise of communism or in a post-capitalist era, this term is a misnomer). It is the task of the whole church. Peter Kusmic articulated it well: "Mission is the task of the whole church—not just a task for a few cross-cultural specialists. The church must discover its missionary nature." The church is the body of Jesus, and He is the head of the church. Jesus is the Missionary. Therefore, in union with Him and as members of the church, every believer has a missionary responsibility.

The 1990 Asia Missions Congress in Seoul, Korea, declared the following goals:

- To commit ourselves to make the Great Commission the primary focus of our personal ministry, and that of the churches and organizations we represent.

- To do all possible to ensure that the cause of world evangelization becomes an integral part of the life of every local church, association of churches, and denomination.

- To mobilize the entire membership of local congregations to pray, give, and send or go, regardless of their economic or political status.

Obviously, this is not just a call to missions. It is a call to evangelical partnership. No one nation is capable of accomplishing the task. The questions are: Will evangelical Christians enter into this partnership? And what kind of partnership will it be? Have we learned from the praises and pains of previous missions experiences? This is more true of Asian missions as we gradually metamorphose from receiving to sending churches. Are we going to be better sending churches? In a sense, I am talking more about ourselves, because some of our missionaries are gaining the notoriety of being worse taskmasters than our "colonial" predecessors.

This presentation is not a documentary of cases. It comes out of personal observations and discussions with many leaders. Most of the discussions deal with partnership in countries where there are established and emerging churches. Obviously, this will be an agenda for missions as they start ministry in countries where there are still no churches. In fact, I am slanting this presentation from an organizational, not a missiological perspective.

This presentation is also predicated on the imperative need to review current church/missions relationship in the light of rapid changes in our times, in a new world of "interlinked economies," in the changing face of Christianity, and in the growing fourth wave of missions—Third World missions! In *Through the Looking Glass*, the Queen said, "It's a poor sort of memory that only works backwards." There is no U-turn on the road to the future. We need to be forward looking in our ministries.

The Issue of Control in Church/Missions Relationship

Was it not Thomas Jefferson who said that there is an aristocrat in every one of us? History reminds us the bitter lesson that the strong control the weak, the rich control the poor, and so on. Sadly, in spiritual matters, we find cases of missions controlling nationals and vice versa. What are some of these critical issues of control that affect church/missions relationship?

1. Misuse of Money

The sub-Christian use of money as power to control in a relationship is a pernicious evil. Money is neutral by itself, but it has an inherent power to corrupt, resulting in abuse. Money is not only a precise valuation of commodities, it is also a measurement of character. It has caused the fall of many godly men and destroyed many working partnerships. As so it is with church/missions partnership.

At the risk of oversimplification and allowing for exceptions, the "carrot and stick" model of missions is too common. Missions dangle the carrot (monetary incentives) in front of the donkey (a grossly inappropriate analogy for church workers). When the donkey takes steps to bite the carrot, the carrot is always moved beyond his reach. Being a donkey, he does not realize the impossibility of his situation. He becomes a slave to his own material needs or greed. And this is supposed to be a motivational approach to get things done by missions!

Translated in blatant terms, many times church workers are bought by newly starting missions. The national denominations cannot compete with the material incentives of higher pay, better benefit packages, and attractive educational offers by these missions. The most promising church workers are oftentimes the target. These workers change camps, creating bitterness and division. Granted that the denomination failed to provide better options for its workers; still, the back-door negotiation hurts. To justify the means by its end of planting churches does not make it Christian. The means must justify itself.

The situation may be avoided if, on one hand, the leaders of the new mission build a relationship with the denominational leaders, present their vision, and seek the following possibilities:

• The new mission could develop a partnership with the denomination to work with them in planting denominational churches (this has worked well in many cases).

• If the new mission is bent on planting its own denominational church, the mission should at least seek the permission of the national church leaders about the plan to employ church workers. There will be reluctance here, but the decision eventually belongs to the workers concerned, and it will gain the respect of the leadership. The ethical consideration will have to be resolved by the new mission itself.

On the other hand, national workers should secure understanding and acceptance from their leaders about their change of ministry. It is always possible that God can lead them to a new place of ministry. They must be a healing force to avoid needless division. There is no need to lose face. When Christ saved us, He gave us back our faces of true humanity and dignity. We should strive for a win/win situation.

When leadership is bought, loyalty will be in question. We deny dignity, just as Jacob did to Esau. When the money supply is gone, there is little commitment to stay. Such a method is costly in cash. One cannot buy self-respect. The principle remains: one reaps what he sows. The danger to the national is the development of a mercenary mentality. Are our services available to the highest bidder?

When money is used to control, missions will hurt. Christ is dishonored. The relationship will deteriorate into either "money with missionary" on the part of the mission or "money without missionary" on the part of the church. Both missionaries and money are needed, but they need not be mutually exclusive. The ultimate question for these missions is: Will they continue to serve the nationals when they can no longer dominate them?

2. Ambiguous Missions Policy

How is the mission agency connected to the church? It is essential that the nature of the local church to be planted be defined by the mission agency. When a church is planted, is it a part of the missionary's home church? Is it going to be an independent national church that becomes a partner of the home church denomination? If the national church is a part of the home church, then it will reflect the missionary's church in theology and doctrines, polity and policy, worship and witness. What happens is a denominational culture transfer from foreign mission to churches, rather than an enrichment of culture in Christ Jesus. Basic theological positions are to be affirmed with deep appreciation, even pride, of one's denominational heritage. But there must be room for the creative expression of one's faith in God in worship, music, and witness.

Some missionaries by their actions do not seem to believe in the centrality and authority of the local church. They show little church loyalty, are free to attend any church, and give their tithes to other agencies but not to the church they are planting. It is as if they are saying to the nationals, "Follow what we tell you; don't follow what we do." There is no clear and common ecclesiology. So even the home church does not know how to relate to the national Christians. The church views these believers as objects or even fruits of mission efforts, but not as fellow members of the church, equal before God. Nationals may not be welcomed in the home church of the missionaries except during missionary conferences. We see today an increasing ethnicity of churches. And if we are not careful, we will experience more and more evangelical *apartheid*. Missions at times can be more interested in evangelism than in the converts as individuals.

A cursory look at the curriculum of Bible colleges for nationals will reveal a duplication of the curriculum of the foreign training program of missionaries. Bible colleges for nationals are designed to meet international accreditation standards, which may be desired if the schools are to produce more relevant workers. But, as in the Philippines for example, very few courses deal with how the church can handle poverty or respond to socio-political issues. Most mission agencies come from a situation which is socio-politically stable. They are not dealing with revolutions or with justice issues, or with people frustrated at their loss of identity and meaning.

Globalization renders a centralized superstructure less and less effective. Communication and technological breakthroughs bring in the information society spoken of by socio-political and management pundits. This means that we are now in the twilight of sovereignty, for even governments are losing control, especially of electronic impulses that bring signals to hand-held cellulars and faxes. In such a situation, people want partnership where each recognizes each other's worth as God's people. This may mean, in the words of Cuno Pumpin, the development of "autonomous sub-systems" or entrepreneurial initiatives which will be the wave of the future.

3. Misuse of Infrastructures

A grave concern emerges when missions start programs or systems that are too expensive for the nationals to take over. Infrastructures that are expensive can be a statement of intent for continuing missions presence and control. The expensive infrastructure that is beyond the ability of the national church to sustain will restrain nationalization of leadership. To avoid this, missions should establish structures that are commensurate with the ability of the nationals themselves to take over, or they should create a partnership based on what each can give in the way of money and manpower. Misuse of the infrastructure takes place when mission funds continue to be funneled to the program or system, even though the leadership has shifted to the nationals.

A "put up or shut up" missions policy for nationals will not provide a good foundation for partnership. Rather, it will hinder the development of national leadership and can degenerate into a dependency syndrome. This will be tragic in the long term. The danger is the backlash of nationalism. The nationals, reacting to such restraining structures, may pursue a hard-line policy against missions. This has happened before in more than one country. The call for moratorium in missions some years ago was a statement of protest. Obviously, expensive infrastructures can be a manipulative strategy to ensure foreign missions leadership. The national leaders are marginalized and the church weakened in its life and witness.

In some cases, missions nationalize leadership of structures. But the danger comes when the leadership is nominal and not real, and the needed financial support to maintain the structure still flows through the missionary. The foreign mission agency becomes a shadow government. Presence and control continue. The golden rule becomes, "He who has the gold, rules." Democracy is a very strange political case of bad arithmetic. In a democracy, 51 percent is 100 percent, and 49 percent is 0 percent. On the other hand, the situation is aggravated by the fact that if money is the voting power, then the vote of 1 with money is 100, and 99 is 0 because there is no money.

4. Cross-Cultural Sensitivity

It is interesting to note that Dr. Met Castillo's practical test for missionary adjustment includes this sensory question: "How is your nose (smell); your tongue (taste); your ear (ability to listen); and your back (ability to sleep anywhere)?" There is truth in the observation that while some missionaries have stayed on the mission field for many years, they have remained monocultural. To cross the cultural divide from one's culture into another requires much "dying." It involves knowing the people and being one with them. Cultural adaptation makes for good communication.

To accomplish this, it is important that the missionary (to use Kenichi Ohmae's term in *The Borderless World*) "denationalize" himself. He slowly divests himself of his cultural baggage, such as, "missionaries are superior in race and ways," "think biggies," "infallible policies," "to be understood rather than understand," etc. This process will most likely lead to a ministry of cultural transfer. The missionary becomes the standard of Christianity. While it is true that Paul said, "Follow me as I follow Christ," we need also to be reminded that even the Holy Spirit does not draw men and women unto Himself but unto Christ.

In his book *Integrity*, Ted Engstrom relates a story by Tom Houston about Alan Redpath's visit to Nairobi in the '60s:

> He had been seeing Africa only through white missionary eyes. One evening I invited a group of black leaders to our home to have a meal with him and Marjorie. As he listened to their perceptive on the mis-

sionary story, he became increasingly frustrated until he burst out and said, "Did we do anything right?"

Then there was a pause, and one man, Daniel Wacko by name, said, "Yes, yes. You did do something right. You gave us the standard by which to judge you. If you had not shown us the truth of Christ, you would not have put yourself to badly in the dark."

This is a powerful story, a warning for modern missions. The philosopher Santayana once said, "Ignorance of history deserves its repetition." Christ is the plumb line to evaluate missions and missionaries.

5. Widening Gap in Technology and Information

Mission work is becoming high-tech in many areas. In an age of information, missions would have an advantage in data gathering. It will have control of needed information for ministry. Information today is fast replacing money as capital, and it will be just as indispensable in planning. If the information gap between missions and nationals widens, the agenda will be dictated by the one who has control of the information.

The need is to enable and to equip national leaders to use technology and process information. There must be information sharing as a prerequisite to "thinking together" in planning. As the saying goes:

> Coming together is a beginning,
> Staying together is progress,
> Thinking together is unity,
> Working together is success.

Technology and information must be brought into the partnership. This means that in countries with established and even emerging churches, missionaries must be prepared to use technology and be computer literate. The future workers must be trained accordingly. They must not only have insights but outsights, capturing the future in the present.

6. Excessive Accountability Requirements

Reports are important, but when the reporting requirements become excessive, they can be a form of control. More time is spent in making reports than in actual ministry. The computers must be satisfied. And the more sophisticated the software program, the more insatiable is the appetite for information. Nationals, unless enabled, just cannot catch up. The situation can result in frustration or in an attitude of resignation that the foreign mission is here to stay. Demotivation to assume leadership occurs. Passivity sets in. Nationals refuse responsibility, simply because they are not responsibly able to meet the impossible demands of reports, computers, and administration.

Effective Control

But is control necessary? Certainly! Peter Senge in *The Fifth Discipline* says, "All healthy organisms have processes of control. However, they are distributed processes, not concentrated in any one authoritarian decision maker."* Control is indispensable in any organization. It is the kind and the exercise of control that is at issue. There are three forms of control that are much more effective than the traditional centralization of power.

1. Shared Vision

Let the expatriate mission leader and the national leader have a shared vision of what they will do in that country and in the rest of the world. In seminars, I encourage leaders of organizations to internalize the essence of their vision and to articulate their vision in one concise sentence. Leaders with visions reinvent themselves to achieve their visions. It is the best form of control because it is self-control.

---

* Senge, P. (1990). *The fifth discipline.* New York: Doubleday.

2. Common Values

Common values can be found whenever the people within foreign missions as well as nationals have common attitudes, such as the following:

- Transparency.
- Readiness to listen to each other.
- Readiness to consult with each other.
- Commitment to do things in a manner consistent with the Word of God and with the laws of the land.

When we are prepared to develop common values about how we do things together as expatriate and national leaders, that set of common values will become part of an internal culture of that denomination or organization, which will again result in the best form of control—self-control.

3. A Good Common Plan

When a common plan exists for both the nationals and the foreign mission, that is the best control, because when you plan, you control. If you really want to control, you plan. The moment you start planning, that control mechanism is there automatically.

A Look Into the Future

1. Change

There is a need to change. "The greatest room in the world," as Chandler McAlpine once said, "is the room for improvement." There is a better way of doing things. To change, we need humility to admit this need. Change requires servant leadership. While there is truth in what G. T. Niles once said, "It is easier to dole out services than to be servants," still we serve a God with whom nothing is impossible. Change begins with ourselves and the truth that we affirm. After all, being precedes doing.

2. Written Agreements

Written agreements are also needed. Even Christians should enter into written agreements! Leaders change, but organizations do not have memories. Continuity requires written agreements. These foster harmony, eliminate wasted time, and avoid needless drain of emotions. To have a working agreement that truly reflects the hearts and minds of foreign missions and nationals, both sides must develop an attitude of seeking to understand the other rather than simply wanting to be understood. Positional unilateral bargaining will not work. Each must listen and labor to know where the other is coming from and what he is saying. Only when a party is certain that what he says is valuable should he put his own values in. This will make him a true partner in the developing partnership. This approach will also result in the common ownership of the agreement, which is the essence of true motivation. These agreements should include the following core commitments:

Statement of Relationship

Expatriate missions (in partnership or at least in dialogue with national leaders, where possible) should develop a clear mission statement articulating their vision and the role of missionaries in a given country. Begin with the end, and from the very start aim at planting a church that is both missionary and prophetic. Do not try to make the church missionary through missionary conventions. Missions is not an addendum but the agenda of the church. A clear mission statement will help avoid moribund missions and missionary frustrations. If missionaries do not know where they are going, as the Cheshire cat told Alice, "It doesn't matter which way you go."

Authority of the Local Church

Develop an ecclesiology that defines the nature of the church, its authority in decision making, and its centrality in missions. In many interviews with foreign missionary candidates, I find that they cannot articulate these issues well.

Answers focus on soul winning but not on the church to nurture those won for Jesus.

Plan of Action

Work on a basic outline for a strategic plan (at least five years), and flesh out the operational plan on a yearly basis in the field. It is best for missions to have a philosophy of ministry wherein the epitome of their achievement is the maturation of national leadership. This will preserve the fruit of missions and provide for continuity in both mission and church. In planning, therefore, mission agencies must begin with the end. And when agencies begin, they must plan to withdraw. Often the scaffolding clings to the building so that it is viewed as part of the building. The seed must fall to the ground if the tree is to grow and bear fruit.

Clear Standard of Performance

An objective performance standard must be jointly established, against which performance evaluation is to be made. Without such a criterion for success, every opinion is as good as the other. This will only absolutize the relative. Mission agencies must not subscribe to the statement, "Truth is on the side of the one who pays the payroll." Such a mindset only creates deep feelings of injustice and undermines organizational integrity.

A performance standard will provide the parties with opportunities for in-progress corrections, should there be variances or deviations in performance. Major mistakes can thus be avoided, and valuable learning exercises that cement relationships can be facilitated.

Capability and Accountability

In order to prosper, partnership must not be paternalistic. While paternalism is recognized in the new birth of the church, expatriate missions must not perpetuate church infancy. To do so stifles growth. Rather, the young church must be allowed to bear the pangs of adolescence unto maturity. Nationals must be allowed to make mistakes. If they do not make mistakes, then they may not be growing or they are not trying their best. Training of national replacements should be a prime agenda of a mission when it starts any ministry. Failure in this area is failure in mentoring and modeling. Missionaries who believe that nationals under their care cannot be trusted have an undue regard of themselves. The Pygmalion principle simply makes their opinion of their wards a self-fulfilling prophecy.

Nationals, on the other hand, must seek to develop competence in management leadership and to be accountable for programs and resources entrusted to them. Accepting responsibility and receiving money without accountability are just as sub-Christian for nationals as the "carrot and stick" policy of missions.

Evangelical Cooperation

Missions should inculcate evangelical unity and cooperation that is transdenominational. The exclusivism of some missions has produced a separatistic mindset. One of the tragic paradoxes in evangelicalism today is the theological reality of the unity of all believers in Christ, contrasted with the fact of their divisions, which are fostered sometimes by agencies and denominationalism.

Missions must learn to work in cooperation with other evangelical groups in the country. In this sense, it is best for all concerned to form a representative national evangelical fellowship or alliance or strengthen an existing one. Such a structure can empower the national evangelicals in their standing before their government, society, and other major religious groups, as well as articulate their voice on critical national issues. This alliance should be their structure for cooperation and communication, so that together they can efficiently use their limited collective resources to effectively disciple the nations for Christ.

In today's world of rapidly shifting paradigms, mission agencies should not be myopic in their task. They must be forward looking and must think in terms of a holistic worldview for the church. They must be clear in their biblical vision for a society in which there is religious liberty for all, a diminishing poverty among the people, and the planting of viable churches in every village and people group in each country.

Final Observations

The issue of control in the ongoing debate about church/missions relationship is critical in our times. One penetrating analysis of the anatomy of control is made by James M. Kouzes and Barry Z. Posner in *The Leadership Challenge*:

> Traditional management thinking promotes the idea that power is a fixed sum: if I have more, then you have less. Naturally, people who hold this view are reluctant to share power. They hold tightly onto what little power they may perceive themselves to have. But this view is archaic, and it seriously retards getting extraordinary things done. Moreover, Rosabeth Moss Kanter has observed that "powerlessness corrupts, and absolute powerlessness corrupts absolutely." People who feel powerless, be they managers or subordinates, tend to hoard whatever shreds of power they have. Powerlessness creates organizational systems where political skills become essential, and "covering" yourself and "passing the buck" become preferred styles for handling inter-departmental differences.*

Such an analysis can easily be true in the power struggle between expatriate missionaries and national leaders. We are reminded of the jockeying for power among the disciples as to who should sit on the right and left side of Jesus in His kingdom. The disciples understood their reward to be privilege and power. Jesus meant service and powerlessness. The focus is not on getting but on giving. It is not on self but on others. A misunderstanding of God's design will create a climate that undermines any authentic partnership in the Lord. True part-

---

* Kouzes, J. M., & Posner, B. Z. (1987). *The leadership challenge.* San Francisco: Jossey-Bass.

nership and sharing are given to us by the Apostle Paul: "At this present time your abundance also may become a supply for their want, that their abundance may become a supply for your want, that there may be equality; as it is written, 'He who gathered much did not have too much, and he who gathered little had no lack'" (2 Cor. 8:14-15). This was the foundation for the Interchurch Relief and Development Alliance (IRDA) of World Evangelical Fellowship when it was established in 1990. It is a timeless principle.

Last January, during the planning session of the managers of the Philippine Council of Evangelical Churches (PCEC) and the Philippine Relief and Development Services (PHILRADS), God impressed upon my heart a special burden. As I looked at the faces of these men, one thought racing through my mind gripped me with such tremendous force that it hurt and even made me frantic. The thought was phrased in two words: "Unfinished business." Had I done all I could to make these men better managers so they could carry out their ministries with greater success after I am gone? It was probably presumptuous on my part to think that I had. But this is a real concern that underscores the role of true leadership.

Then, as if to reinforce the message, shortly after those seminars, during my birthday fellowship attended by friends and colleagues in ministry, my children offered a song for me. As they sang, I was lost in time. My mind was desperately screaming a question: "Are they singing the song from the depths of their hearts, not because they must please me for the occasion but because it is the conviction of their beings?" The chorus asserted:

> You'll never know that you're our hero,
> You're everything we would like to be,
> We can fly higher than an eagle,
> Because you are the wind beneath our wings.

Position and possessions did not matter then. All I could think was "unfinished business." Have I done all I could to raise my children in the words and ways of the Lord?

The very essence of church/missions partnership should be the glory of God. But if I may ask for a very human goal, it is precisely the joy of seeing the transition of foreign missions to the national church and its national leaders. Success in missions is not a solo marathon race. It is the timely handing of the baton to the next runner. Let us run the race together unto the furtherance of the gospel.

Until then, my friends, let us forge a partnership that is grounded in the gospel, demonstrating the gospel, unto the furtherance of the gospel. Let us capture God's strategic moments today and work synergistically for His glory. Amen.

Jun (or JV) Vencer is a Filipino lawyer and pastor. From 1978 to 1993, he was the General Secretary of the Philippine Council of Evangelical Churches. Concurrently he was the General Director of the Philippine Relief and Development Services, and he served as Chairman of DAWN for the Philippines. In 1992 he was elected International Director of World Evangelical Fellowship. Married to Annabella, he has four children.

10

Confidence Factors: Accountability in Christian Partnerships

Alexandre Araujo

The primary purpose of this paper is to address account-ability not only as a necessary but also as a positive component of a healthy partnership. Accountability can be applied to strengthen a partnership by identifying things that threaten the partnership and proposing ways in which the threat can be initially avoided or removed. It need not be seen as a cold, critical evaluation of a partner, but as a tool for enhancing the success of the partnership.

The approach of confidence factors discussed below works in both directions. Either partner can use these factors as a means of assessing its own confidence in the other—a confidence without which no partnership can succeed. This approach can be easily adaptable to a variety of circumstances and can provide some concrete measurements of the strength and stability of a partnership.

Accountability and Culture

If we are going to talk about accountability in Christian partnerships, we must first overcome a popular misconception that accountability is geographically and culturally bound. In

119

fact, we often imply, with great inaccuracy, that accountability is a Western concept—that somehow Korean churches grow without accountability, that Brazilians train and send cross-cultural missionaries without it, that the Evangelical Mission-ary Society of Nigeria can train and deploy over 800 missionaries without any concept of accountability. The day is fast approaching when we will no longer need to conceive of the world of missions as divided between West and non-West. It is already nearly impossible to talk about partnership in missions without thinking of cooperative working relation-ships between Christians from both sides of the divide. There-fore, if we believe that accountability is a necessary element of healthy partnerships, we must abandon any trace of belief that it is primarily a Western concept.

The concept of accountability is a universal concept. It is also biblical. We find it in Genesis 3, where God calls on Adam and Eve to account for their choices and actions. Cain was held accountable by God for his actions concerning his brother, and God would hold accountable anyone who would threaten Cain's life. People have been held accountable from the begin-ning of time—to God, to local government, to parents and patriarchs, to spouses. In fact, accountability seems to be essential to any meaningful relationship between persons in all cultures. It may be called different things and described in different ways by different cultures, but the concept is there all the same.

Defining Accountability

Accountability in its broadest sense is the condition whereby one person is subject to review, examination, and judgment by another person or authority structure concerning his or her motives and actions. This is often involuntary, in the sense that I do not have a choice but to be accountable. There is a sense in which I am "my brother's keeper," that I am accountable for what happens to other believers, and for how my life affects others. God or civil authorities will hold us accountable to fulfill their expectations of us, whether or not we agree. The purpose of this paper, however, is to discuss a more specific type of accountability, that which is applicable to Christian partnerships.

Accountability in Christian Partnerships

Accountability in Christian partnerships is a willingness to place oneself under someone else's review and examination concerning one's motives, actions, and outcomes according to mutually agreed upon expectations, in an environment of good faith and mutual trust.

Notice that accountability in Christian partnerships goes further than general accountability in that it is voluntary, and it is based on good faith and mutual trust. While commitments made in this context are just as binding as in any other, in Christian partnerships there is the added element of a good attitude towards accountability itself. Accountability is welcomed as a blessing rather than being viewed as a restrictive imposition.

Mutual Trust, Not Control

Since the success of partnerships depends on each partner's capability to fulfill its part of the agreement, it is essential that we evaluate our partner's capabilities as well as our own. When two parties agree to work together toward a specific and clearly defined goal, it is not sufficient that they have good intentions. They must also be capable of doing what they have committed to do.

Often one partner will seek to compensate for its lack of confidence in the other by exercising control over the partnership. A mission organization in a given country may involve national believers in its work, but it may retain all the decision-making power for fear that the national believers may not know what to do or how to do it. In other words, the mission organization lacks confidence in nationals' capability, even if it trusts their motives and dedication. For a long time in the history of modern missions, this difficulty on the part of many Western missionaries to develop confidence in their national brothers and sisters has led them to retain control.

It is very difficult to relinquish control without having first gained confidence in our partners. Yet, if we are to honor each other in the Lord, *we must be willing to seek those conditions that allow us to abandon the urge to control in exchange for a well-founded confidence in each other.* This does not mean that we abandon our desire to do a good job "as unto the Lord." It does mean that we stop viewing our partners as extensions of ourselves, existing only to fulfill *our* program. Instead, we must start viewing them as godly men and women in their own right, with equal access to the Father and equally capable of hearing His voice. We may disagree with them, but if we lack sufficient confidence in their capabilities, it is better to forsake a formal working partnership, which requires commitment to specific tasks and objectives, and preserve the bond of fellowship in the Spirit, which allows spontaneous cooperation with one another without the strict mutual expectations that a working partnership requires.

It is crucial that questions of control and accountability be identified and dealt with openly at the beginning of the partnership. The initial negotiation must be done in good faith. There should be no sense that a partner is doing the other a favor by agreeing to work together. Unless both partners believe that they need each other, the partnership will be one-sided and is open to tensions and misunderstandings.

Accountability Without Control Involves Risk

If we cannot control our partner, how can we be assured of our partner's ability or commitment to fulfill obligations of the partnership? Is it wrong to expect our partner to meet certain standards of quality and performance? Of course not! Partnerships are based on clearly defined expectations on both sides, and it is quite appropriate for each partner to hold the other accountable for commitments made.

Is it possible to guarantee quality and good performance without control? The answer is a resounding NO! In a partnership it is not possible for one partner to guarantee or assure good performance by the other. Partnership between two autonomous entities involves a certain amount of risk. This may be the reason that, in the recent history of Western missions, it has been preferable to establish field branches which are extensions of, and therefore controllable by, the parent agency, rather than to turn over leadership to the local believers. (The ironic thing is that Western control does not ensure quality either! Examples abound.)

In a partnership, we must be prepared for the possibility that our partner may fall short of our expectations. But if we cannot resort to control in order to prevent failure, is there any way to avoid entering into a partnership blindly? Don't we have a responsibility to be good stewards of the resources given to us to administer? A healthy partnership is founded on the ability to have confidence in one another. I must be able to trust that you, my partner, are both willing to, and capable of, fulfilling your part. And you must also be able to trust me.

But how do I differentiate between trust and irresponsibility? Responsible trust is based on my confidence in your ability to do your part, and vice versa. And we acquire confidence in one another by making certain objective observations about how each of us conducts our affairs. I cannot control you, but I can observe how you work and draw my conclusions. What I know about your thinking and planning concerning your share in the partnership determines the level of my confidence in your ability to fulfill your part. And you, of course, will do the same with me. *Good will and positive thinking cannot replace the confidence that is based on objective knowledge of each other's capabilities and basic plans for using those capabilities.*

Partnership Is Built on Mutual Expectations

A partnership is built around clearly identified mutual expectations and can be defined as *a working relationship between two or more autonomous entities whereby each contributes, by mutual agreement, some of its own resources, according to mutually established and clearly defined expectations, toward the accomplishment of a common goal.*

I must know specifically what you will contribute to the partnership, and you also must know what to expect of me. Our confidence in one another then is not simply a general good feeling toward one another but rather an informed assessment that, concerning the specific set of expectations that form our partnership, we have confidence in one another. This is true in complex partnerships just as much as in a simple prayer partnership between two people.

A simple illustration will help clarify what we mean by clearly defined expectations. Let us say that a Western agency wants to translate the Bible for a certain language group within a closed country. While it cannot place its own translators there, it can provide training for Christian members of that language group so they in turn can translate the Bible. It is not sufficient that there is good Christian fellowship between the Western missionaries and the national Christian leaders. Specific expectations must be developed. What would they be?

The national church may expect the following from the Western agency:

- That it will provide the trainers.

- That the trainers will be competent linguists.

- That the trainers will respect the national organization's autonomy.

The Western agency may expect of the national church:

- That the church will provide competent trainees.

- That they will develop a plan to do Bible translation once the training is completed.

- That the translation skills will be used for Bible translation.

Other expectations may be stated concerning specific tasks, a timetable, channels of communication between the partners, etc. Once these and other related expectations are identified, each partner assesses its confidence in the other's capability and intent to fulfill expectations.

It is true that our confidence may disappoint us. As we said before, we cannot guarantee that the other partner will fulfill its part. All we can do is obtain enough confidence that our partner intends to do so and also is capable of doing so.

An Important Caution

We must make the distinction between confidence in persons and confidence in an organization or operation. For instance, suppose I need eye surgery. I have a friend who is honest, courteous, kind, and humble. The fruit of the Spirit is evident in his life. He is very concerned with my plight and would like to do something about it. But if he offers to take care of my eye surgery, being godly is not enough. I want evidence that he is qualified as an eye surgeon. In other words, though I may respect him *personally*, I need to look for those factors that give me confidence in him *professionally*.

It is important to understand that we are not passing judgment on a brother or sister as such, but only on his or her capability to do what he or she has committed to do in the specific confines of the partnership agreement.

Confidence Factors

Concerning missions, when we talk about partnerships, we are typically thinking about a cooperative working arrangement between two or more Christian organizations or agencies. Since our confidence must be based on a solid foundation, what are some practical ways in which partners can establish confidence in each other? Let me propose six factors that help determine whether or not I can trust that my partner's organization can meet mutually agreed upon expectations.

1. Internal Accountability Structure

Does the organization have an internal accountability structure (such as a board of directors or executive committee) that is *informed*, *involved*, and *responsible* for the ministry?

Informed: Board members know the leaders and workers, the goals and objectives of the ministry, the more significant program activities, the status of finances, and the accounting procedures. They know the more significant administrative procedures and who is responsible for major decisions. They are able to explain and promote the ministry to others.

Involved: Board members attend board meetings regularly and assume responsibility for decisions of policy. They pray faithfully for the ministry and its leaders and workers, visit ministry locations occasionally, and have some degree of first-hand knowledge of the ministry.

Responsible: Board members see themselves as ultimately responsible for the ministry. When there are problems, they step in and do their part to resolve them. They support the ministry financially or in other ways. They are legally responsible for the ministry.

A board that does these things provides stability and helps preserve the sense of direction of the ministry and its leaders. It provides an accountability structure for ministry leaders and protects the credibility of the ministry before the rest of the evangelical community, the public authorities, and society in general.

It should be noted that this accountability structure does not need to be something very complicated. It can be a very structured, formal board of directors of the kind found in large, complex organizations, but it can also be an informal group of mature men and women who meet regularly and who assume personal and corporate responsibility for the integrity of the ministry and its leaders.

2. Clear, Measurable, and Achievable Goals and Objectives

Are the organization's goals and objectives clear, measurable, and achievable?

Clear: Goals and objectives should be easy for ministry staff to understand, fully embrace, and explain to others, especially to their partners.

Measurable: It must be possible to measure progress in achieving the goals. For instance, if a ministry wants to plant 10 churches, then criteria must exist which define when a church is planted. What are the ingredients of a functioning church? How are these ingredients being measured? Whatever the goal, progress toward that goal must be measurable.

Achievable: Goals and objectives should be things that a ministry can actually hope to accomplish. For example, the goal "to reach the lost with the gospel" is not adequate. Every Christian organization can say the same thing. An achievable goal is more specific, naming target groups, numbers, time-frames, and methods. Each ministry's specifics will be different and can be very simple or very complex, but the goals need to be achievable.

3. Policies and Procedures

Does the organization have specific policies and procedures to guide staff in areas such as program operations and financial management?

Policies: Policies define the principles that will govern the organization. They define the authority structure, how decisions are made, and by whom. Every organization, no matter how small or how simple, needs to define its policies.

Procedures: Procedures describe the mechanism for implementing policies: who does what task, what records must be kept, etc.

Program: There must be policies and procedures which assure that the ministry is being developed in accordance with the purpose, goals, and objectives of the organization.

Finances: The policies and procedures must be adequate to assure that funds are being spent in accordance with designations and are being accurately accounted for. An example of a financial policy is that all financial decisions must be approved by the board of directors. A specific procedure might be that requests for expenses will be submitted by the director to the board treasurer for approval once a month.

4. Adequate Personnel

Does the organization have personnel adequate in number and skills to accomplish the goals and objectives of the partnership? Unless an organization has the people to do the work, the work will not be done. Unless the people have the needed skills, the work will not be done properly. For instance, an organization may have the best policies and procedures for financial management, but if it does not have someone who can keep good accounting records, it will not be able to adequately do the work to meet expectations.

5. Credibility

Does the organization have credibility with the evangelical community? If those who know the partner the most cannot recommend it without reservations, we would do well to reconsider our intent to establish a partnership. We would do well to research our potential partner's credibility within its own working environment, especially if we are from a different culture. It is possible for us, coming from the outside, to add tension to local relationships by not paying heed to what responsible local observers can tell us.

6. Past Performance

Has the organization adequately met previous commitments? Good performance of past commitments may be a good indicator of a partner's capability to fulfill its partnership commitments.

How Are Confidence Factors Used?

Notice that the confidence factors listed here are not instruments for control of the partner. They do not tell a partner what to do. The partner leaders, together with their board, decide what goals, objectives, policies, and procedures should be adopted. We simply look for signs that give us confidence that the partner will be able to fulfill expectations. If funds are requested for a project, for instance, we need to have reasonable confidence that the means are in place to ensure correct use of the funds and to provide the necessary financial reports.

We may also use confidence factors to help each other identify areas of strength and of weakness. Using confidence factors in this way will depend, of course, on whether or not the partner leaders want this kind of help. But if they do, the confidence factors will provide a tool to analyze an organization and determine where it needs strengthening. We should be willing to help strengthen each other's weak areas, as long as we don't force our ways on the other nor slip into an attitude of trying to control each other.

Isn't this approach too restrictive? Where are the freedom to follow the Lord's lead and the flexibility to change course along the way? First of all, in a partnership, partners should feel free to discuss and negotiate changes with each other along the way. Partnerships need not be rigid, unbending, legalistic commitments. But what makes a partnership a partnership is that two or more parties voluntarily agree to be bound to each other in those areas that make up the partnership. They agree not to make unilateral decisions or changes in the terms of the agreement. Partnership is nothing more than a question of the integrity of one's word.

Secondly, if I want to preserve my freedom to move unhindered and without having to accommodate another's concerns, I can do so by avoiding relationships that require commitment to others. No one should be forced into a partnership. But if I voluntarily choose to enter into a partnership, I must honor my commitments to my partner and work to earn the partner's confidence, not only in my intent but also in my capability to do what I committed myself to do.

Alex Araujo is the Director of International Operations for Partners International, San Jose, California. Born and raised in Brazil, he was the national director for Brazil for COMIBAM '87, the first continent-wide missions conference for Latin America. Prior to that, he was a missionary in Portugal, and he also served with a prison ministry. Mr. Araujo has a master's degree in political science and worked for several years in municipal government in the USA. As a member of the missions committee of a large church, he provided orientation and introductory training to missions candidates.

Part Three: Internationalizing Agencies

11

Challenges of Partnership: Interserve's History, Positives and Negatives

James Tebbe
Executive Director, Interserve (International Office)
and Robin Thomson
Regional Representative, Interserve (India)

Partnership in mission springs from the biblical perspective of worldwide mission. The world belongs to God, and so our mission is to the whole of His world. This call is given to every church in every place. Each is given the privilege and responsibility of sharing the good news with the whole world, beginning "from Jerusalem...." So every church should be involved in giving and receiving help in this worldwide task.

This beautiful, intricate pattern of equality and mutuality can be seen in the New Testament, especially in Paul's missionary strategy and practice. The pattern has not always been evident since then, either because of lack of spiritual vision or because of economic, political, or social constraints. But in our day it is happening again, on a worldwide scale—a fulfillment of God's plan to demonstrate His "multicolored wisdom" to the whole universe through the church (Eph. 3:9-11). If this means anything, it surely means that God intends the gospel not only to be received by people of every color and race and tribe and language, but also to be carried by them. This in itself will be a demonstration of the universal Lordship of Christ in a world where competing creeds and ideologies claim universal allegiance.

So partnership is an inescapable part of the gospel. But it immediately raises questions. Partnership is between equals who respect each other. But the church today is so diverse—culturally, theologically, socially, economically. It is much easier to see the inequalities. Is it worth the effort of extra communication, structural and financial adjustments, and constant coordination, in order to express what may be only an appearance of equality? The effort to express partnership is based on the universality and equality of the church. But what about its diversity? What about the need for expressing self-hood and identity, especially for a new church, still discovering itself in relation to others? Too close a partnership with a more dominant church might hinder its development or stifle its creativity, like David trying to fight in Saul's armor.

These theological and practical reflections are necessary as we think about partnership. Otherwise we may be frustrated by unrealistic expectations or settle for uneasy coexistence.

One lesson that seems clear is that true partnership, which respects each other's identity and contribution, may have to be expressed in different ways at different times. This has certainly been true in the history of Interserve's efforts to develop partnership.

History and Development
of the Concept of "Partner" in Interserve

Interserve (Indian Female Normal School and Instruction Society) began in the Indian subcontinent in 1852 as a women's mission, serving first in the area of teaching and later in medical work. In the 1950s the first men joined the Society, and in the mid-1960s Interserve (then called the Bible and Medical Missionary Fellowship or BMMF) divested itself of the property and institutions over which it exercised ownership and control, turning them over to local churches and boards. Thus the Fellowship moved from a position of running institutions to that of serving in them.

One reason for the change of name from BMMF to International Service Fellowship (Interserve) in 1986 was to reflect this change of ethos in the organization. At the International Council meeting where the name change was finally decided, the inclusion of "mission" or "missionary" in the new name was carefully considered and then rejected. Security for working in "creative access countries" was one consideration, but the other and, in fact, the major reason was that Interserve no longer was a "missionary society" in the sense of running its own institutions and programs.

In 1987, there was another change in terminology, where a missionary of Interserve became a "Partner" in the Fellowship, rather than a "member." It was felt this was a better term for the agency-to-individual relationship. This could also help Partners of Interserve in their understanding of themselves in creative access countries. This change of terminology from missionary to Partner was a part of Interserve's attempt to define its role in world mission. Partnership is by no means the only dimension to mission, but it is one which Interserve considers important. The word "missionary" has been and can continue to be a helpful label, but Interserve's moving away from that label is indicative of what it feels its contribution should be in the last part of the 20th century.

In 1989 (modified in 1990 and again in 1992), a document entitled "Common Commitment of Partners" was adopted by the Fellowship. Its purpose was to define Interserve's unity and commitment amidst the increasing diversity of locations and financial relationships within the Fellowship. While the primary impetus for the development of the document came from the need to define the relationship of a self-supported "tentmaker" with the Fellowship, the scope was much broader. Some of the concepts presented in Interserve's Common Commitment of Partners relate directly to the subject for this paper and are included in various forms below.

Partnership in the Organizational Structure of Interserve

Organizationally, Interserve is a federation of "National Councils." Each has its own autonomy but has agreed constitutionally to be united together in ministry in Interserve's defined fields of service. Interserve does not have a "General Director" or a "Headquarters." Rather, it has an International Office and Executive Director (International Office)—not to be confused with the Executive Director for each National Council. This International Office acts more as a liaison than headquarters for its National Councils.

At present there are seven National Councils. Also represented are seven "National Committees," the aim of which is to eventually meet the requirements to become National Councils. These National Committees are in both Europe and Asia. In addition to National Committees, there are two other established national agencies (non-Interserve) which recruit and send personnel through Interserve: DMG in Germany and Malaysian CARE. Thus, some of the strengths and struggles of partnership are in Interserve's very organizational structure.

The development of Interserve National Committees is one aspect of the organizational structure worth considering. The question Interserve has asked and continues to ask is, "Why inclusion rather than encouraging an indigenous effort to begin?" In fact, one of the major strategies of the Fellowship is to encourage the development of indigenous missions. There are several ways in which Interserve has taken a proactive role in this area. One example is the partnership agreement with the Indian Evangelical Mission (IEM) to facilitate placement of IEM's personnel outside India. Malaysian CARE and DMG have chosen to work as partner groups rather than adopting an Interserve structure.

On the other hand, there is also the expressed desire of some to be linked with an international organization. Thus, in some instances, after careful consideration, Interserve has become involved in encouraging the development of an Interserve National Committee. Singapore, Hong Kong, and, most recently, Korea are three countries where National Committees of Interserve are presently functioning. Interserve is committed on a course of action to further develop these committees. (There is a separate case study on India below.)

Singapore

In the case of Singapore, originally there was an agreement with Overseas Missionary Fellowship (OMF) to screen and second to Interserve personnel who were called to areas where Interserve had a field structure. In time, OMF recommended and offered assistance in Interserve's setting up its own National Committee. This has happened. Facilitation of this has come from the International Office. But more importantly, it seems that the policy of establishing a link with a particular National Council (in this case, New Zealand) was especially appreciated. Informal links, visits, sharing, encouragement, and some financial help resulted from this relationship. However, there have been some struggles, and the Committee still has not been able to move ahead with a strong flow of personnel.

Hong Kong

Hong Kong also has an Interserve National Committee, and the National Office link has been with Interserve's Australian National Council. Here is a good example of an international versus a national identity. Excellent candidates have recently come forward, but in at least two instances the informal network of churches that would support these candidates wonders about the wisdom of being linked with a foreign organization as 1997 approaches. This concern may arise from the problem the Roman Catholic Church had in China, because of the authority the government perceived came from the Vatican. This network of churches is concerned that it be able to continue after China takes over. It is possible Interserve may continue to develop in Hong Kong. On the other hand, its role may be only to facilitate the beginning of an independent mission. The strengths of an international network, input, and contacts must be weighed against the need not to be seen as a foreign organization.

Korea

In Korea, Interserve took the initiative but was also invited to send speakers and give input into the growing mission awareness of the Korean church. Again, OMF preceded and advised Interserve to set up its own National Committee. In December 1990, Interserve was officially established as an organization in Korea. Short termers have come, and now longer term Partners are expected to be on location by the summer of 1992. Quick development has taken place because a strong lead came from a particular young Korean leader. The National Council to link with Korea was the United States National Council.

Current Challenges

When it comes to the incorporation of National Committees, a major challenge Interserve faces is how to develop a partnership of equality in which the beginning, smaller voice is well heard. It seems the goodwill is there to facilitate this, but the problem is a structural one. For instance, at present our International Council meets once every four years, and the International Executive meets annually. National Councils are officially represented on the Council and Executive, while the Committees are not. Committee representatives are co-opted to the quadrennial International Council meetings, but not to the Executive. The April 1992 meetings were the first in which National Committees were invited to have a representative at the International Executive. Recent discussions in the 1992 International Executive Committee meetings further clarified what it means to be a National Council and the transitional steps from Committee to Council. It seems this change from Committee to Council is probably going to happen sooner rather than later for several of the Committees. This would mean representation on the International Executive Committee. The problem is that as the Executive is expanded, it becomes increasingly unwieldy and unable to do its job. Interserve is trying hard to move away from operating exclusively on Western missiological models, where non-Westerners within the Fellowship can be orphans. But as yet, the voice from the non-Westerners does not have a sufficiently strong base to be automatically included in policy decisions.

Another problem area is that of style—pastoral care as perceived, directives versus suggestions, accountability, etc. Style is a hard enough issue within the diversity of different Western nationalities. Adding a range of non-Western cultures presents further challenges.

Language should not be missed as an area of concern. Interserve has the common language of English. It is required that all adults have reasonably good English. Yet in some countries, children are being educated in local or at least non-English system schools. Right now this is an issue for some of our Partners from Holland who are working in Tunisia, which has a French schooling system. As a result, the children may not develop spoken English. This can inhibit the sense of belonging to Interserve, particularly at key times like conferences, when there are special programs for children.

Interserve's Participation in Partnership Arrangements

Interserve is not a funding organization. Its primary contribution is in the placement of personnel in strategic positions. These positions are not in Interserve structures. In principle, the only Interserve people who work directly for Interserve are those in the administration. Even with administration, in many cases an Interserve Partner does this as a spare-time job. Thus, in a very real sense, virtually every Interserve Partner is a partner in mission with some other group or organization. This partnership has taken several different forms in Interserve. Obviously, sometimes the ideal is different from the practice.

1. Agency Sends Money; Nationals Do Job

One model of partnership involves an agency sending the money and the national church or Christian agency in the country doing the job, whether it be in development or church planting. The name "partner agency" has taken the place of the older term "donor agency" in an effort to remove the concept of inequality that can come with the latter. As Interserve is not a funding agency, nor a denomination with a ready access to a predetermined constituency, nor has a large legacy of funding, it has only been involved in such a partnership arrangement in small, time-limited projects. Interserve has a Leadership Endowment Fund, a Mission Partnership Fund, and a Theological Scholarship Fund. One example of how such money was used was when a certain sum, in decreasing amounts over three years, was given to a specific church to help fund a youth pastor. The expectation was that during that time funding would be found locally to enable this to be an ongoing ministry. The effort was successful, but it was found that expectations needed to be again communicated and the time frame extended. In such instances, hard work needs to be done to maintain an equality and harmony in partnership. This principle of trying to remove the inequality of relationships is an issue Interserve struggles with in other areas of partnership as well.

2. Missionaries Work Under National Structures

Another model of partnership is for mission personnel to come under national structures in the countries where they come to serve. Many mainline denominations have gone this route in putting their personnel directly under the national church. There is no separate organization for the mission. They do not have a conference with a business meeting. Even with funding, in many cases the national church is given the funds, and it in turn pays the missionaries.

A further development to this model is with missionaries coming under a national mission agency. IEM in India is expecting a person from South Africa to come and work directly under them. There is also great potential for this in the case of Christian non-government organizations (NGOs). In the countries with which I am familiar, this approach is only beginning to be considered.

In practice, Interserve has seconded personnel to a national church for an agreed project or job. Additionally, in at least one instance, a person has been seconded to a large Christian NGO (in Egypt). In practice, these secondments have been quite successful, particularly in India, where the Fellowship has a history of service.

Interserve's ideal is to second to local, national organizations. In practice, a number of secondments, and in some places even the majority, are to another expatriate-led organization or in some cases even a mission structure. There are several possible justifications: the particular job is important, there is pressure on Interserve to "place" applicants, there is a visa slot, etc. But the purpose of a structural change in the mid-1950s was to move away from being a "mission"; thus, this type of placement is generally not considered the ideal, but is accepted as necessary.

In seconding personnel, Interserve seeks to maintain at least supplementary pastoral care for its Partners. Secondment is not placing individuals with another group and then having little or no further contact with them during the course of that secondment. Partners still are linked with Interserve and among other things would, for instance, normally attend an annual conference.

As in any situation, however, there can be problems in secondment. On the one hand, a person can feel very alone in a secondment and at times unsupported, coming from a very different culture and perhaps not understanding fully how the organization to which he or she is seconded really works.

On the other hand, perhaps a more common problem is that Interserve fails to recognize the true meaning of the secondment. Because it pays its Partner, provides an infrastructure for pastoral care, has an accountability structure, and is sometimes more efficiently organized, it can fail to treat the secondment as a true secondment. Part of the reason may be that Interserve, according to its policies, usually does not have an organization-to-organization relationship with the churches or groups to which it seconds its Partners. Thus the concept of partnership at that level is not developed. Interserve's policy has been to seek secondments at the level of the local church or organization and not with the sometimes more distant administration. Thus, a secondment is seen as a "local" arrangement. In some cases, it has become necessary to have a formal link with an overall structure, but that usually has proved unnecessary. Of course, in the case of secondment to a national denomination, where appropriate that secondment is organized through the official channels. Interserve has found that a written document signed by the Partner, Interserve, and the receiving organization is usually important to make sure there is a clarity of expectations.

3. United Mission Efforts

Another model of partnership is where Interserve has gone into a united mission effort, such as the United Mission to Nepal or the International Assistance Mission. Agency representation takes place at the Board level, and personnel become full members of the united mission. There is no need for separate secondment agreements, as the organization is set up in such a way as to cover that area. In fact, this model of partnership seems to be a comfortable fit for Interserve. It is in these united efforts that Interserve has been the most successful in recruiting and maintaining personnel. Where there is a local church, the united mission then relates to that body. Apart from individual Partners' ministry and service, Interserve's contribution to the relationship is through its voice on the Board. This approach has been policy and a strong thrust of Interserve in recent years. The Fellowship seeks to maintain active participation on the Boards of these organizations.

4. Networking With Other Organizations

Yet another way in which a partnership is formed is in networking with other organizations. This has been found to be particularly helpful for creative access countries where Interserve has self-supported Partners. There are several different networking groups that meet in Cyprus, in which Interserve has representation. Several have led to the organization of joint programs, such as conferences for tentmakers, refugee relief effort, joint action on issues of social justice, etc.

Because of Interserve's intent to not exist as a "mission" (in the sense of a strong, distinct identity with its own programs and institutions), it has been less involved in the formation of partnerships on the model that has recently developed in North Africa. A strong organizational agenda and unique constituency can lead to the need to have a separate identity. Interserve seems to have gravitated more towards a joint mission arrangement, where it agrees to work under the confines (and strengths!) of a united mission structure.

Having described several of the ways Interserve is involved in partnership, I feel the need to use first person pronouns. We do have strategies, we do have agendas, and we do not always consult or hear another's perspective as broadly as we should. Sometimes the question, "How can we cooperate?" is only a way of saying, "How can you help us do our thing which we have already decided?" Perhaps the international and interdenominational aspect of Interserve helps in softening a strong or narrow agenda, but still as we look at our organizational structure, there is much that could change.

Case Study From India

One topic that might be of the most interest to this consultation would be that of the development of Interserve (India). All in one country, Interserve has the following:

- An agreed partnership arrangement with the Indian Evangelical Mission.

- An Interserve "field" structure which has both Indian and non-Indian Partners.

- A National Committee (now two years old).

Radical Change

The big change came after the first 100 years—not so much the introduction of men as the decision to hand over all institutions and disperse to work in partnership with churches and other groups. Some institutions were closed, while others were handed over to an independent Trust set up to run them. These were radical steps.

Working Together

However, the spirit of partnership was already in existence. The expatriate missionaries in those institutions had already been working side by side with Indian colleagues, some in senior positions. It was natural to invite them to continue as members of BMMF, though working under the new Trust. An Indian Auxiliary of BMMF was formed, along the lines of the earlier auxiliaries formed in Australia, New Zealand, and Canada (which had turned into National Councils). There were about a dozen Indian members, coming from the common institutional past of the Fellowship. Some moved out of the institutions into new ministries.

Partnership Through Secondment

The main thrust, for new and existing workers, was to second them to work with churches and other groups, in strategic ministries such as evangelism, pastoral care, student work, literature work, theological education, or medical work. New relationships were developed with the leadership of these organizations, many new themselves. Some were still led by expatriates, but a new generation of Indian leadership was emerging, especially in student work and theological education. BMMF missionaries worked with and under this leadership, often pioneering new ventures together. They developed close relationships, with high mutual regard, accountability, and communication on the whole. A missionary would not automatically be invited back to work with that group, unless it was acceptable to both sides.

Partnership Through Counsel

The overall leadership of the Fellowship also kept in close touch and consultation with a trusted circle of acknowledged Indian evangelical leaders, who by the 1960s had been invited to form an Advisory Committee. Discussion began to take place about developing this into an "Indian Council" of the Fellowship, to recruit and deploy Indian members. The Indian Council would, in principle, be like other Councils of the Fellowship.

However, this development came to an abrupt halt, around 1970, when the Indian leaders advised that they felt this was not the right direction. It would stifle the development of a genuinely Indian missionary movement, just beginning to grow.

The leaders of BMMF took this advice. No Indian Council was formed, and the Advisory Committee did not function much longer formally, although close consultation continued informally. Some new Indian members had been recruited in the '60s and early '70s, working within India, mostly in disciple making and Bible teaching ministries. But the number of Indian members was never more than about a dozen, and there was a virtual moratorium on their recruitment from the mid-'70s to the mid-'80s.

The Indian missionary movement was growing vigorously meanwhile, mostly in direct evangelistic work, with an emphasis on the unreached tribal populations of North and Central India. BMMF was also growing vigorously, through secondments to a wide spectrum of churches and agencies, almost entirely Indian led. Partnership was strong and in some cases very creative, leading to new ventures, including theological education by extension (TEE) and the first missionary training program, in partnership with the Indian Evangelical Mission.

So partnership during this phase—about 30 years—was best expressed by cooperation through secondment and networking. Note that this was not the result of inability or unwillingness to work more closely together, but rather the reverse. As a result of open communication and mutual respect, it was agreed that this was the best form of partnership. Partnership was greatly helped by the fact that BMMF had no churches, institutions, or property of its own—and not very large funds either. In this regard, BMMF was perceived to be significantly different from many other groups.

At the same time, this arrangement left BMMF free to make its own decisions as to which groups it would cooperate with and how it would deploy its members. Counsel was sought and received through Asian involvement in International and Asia level Councils and Committees. This counsel was genuine and was taken seriously, but it was essentially consultancy. There was no executive involvement by Indians or any other Asians in the leadership. BMMF was international, but is was definitely Western international. Some people were comfortable with this composition, while others felt it a deficiency that needed to be corrected. But change did not seem to be possible in the short term, with the emphasis on allowing Indian organizations, and especially missions, the freedom to develop on their own. Serious thought was given to ways to help develop Asian missions, but the effort to find new Asian involvement in BMMF was largely channeled to other Asian countries, as noted earlier in this paper.

Radical Change Again?

In 1984, change was forced on the leadership by the Indian government's new, much tighter visa policy. This meant a drastic reduction in the number of expatriate BMMFers in India and eventually led to the relocation of the International Office from India to Cyprus in 1985.

What did this mean for the future of BMMF in India? Some felt strongly that it was time to recognize the end of an era and move on to new challenges in other regions. Others were not so sure. Two parallel moves were made in response to the new situation. One was to set up a holding trust, with all Indian members, to provide the legal and financial cover for BMMF to continue in India. This was essentially an administrative response to keep in existence, with no necessary implication of future development. The other move was a call from some of the members of BMMF in India to see the situation as the end of a chapter but the opportunity to open a new chapter, in which BMMF in India would become an even closer part of the Indian missionary movement, both receiving and sending missionaries from outside and inside India.

The proposal led to a lively debate within the Fellowship, inside and outside India. Many were not sure, while others felt these reservations were illegitimate nostalgia for the past, based on a sense of bereavement. Other Indian missions, represented in the Councils of the Fellowship, also questioned the idea. Why not continue the existing models of partnership? To try to become an Indian mission would lead to unnecessary duplication and even competition.

The Vision for Interserve (India)

The debate continued for several months, with Indian and expatriate voices on both sides. But by early 1987, the members of Interserve (as it now was) working in India felt sure that God was calling them to form a new body. It would be distinctively Indian but also international. It would have explicit continuity with Interserve/BMMF of the past. It would continue to receive but also send missionaries. It should become a National Committee of the Fellowship and eventually a National Council.

Why not just continue the existing models of partnership? Indian Partners felt that these models need not be affected. But India had changed. The church, and Indian missions in particular, had developed maturity and confidence. There had been tremendous growth in outreach and mission. But there was still room—and a definite need—for Interserve's distinctive contributions and style of work. (These were defined by some as including the principle of secondment, holistic ministry, leadership "from the middle," international ethos, and genuine partnership of mutual respect.) Interserve should continue to contribute to the Indian church's mission, along with the others, and should help to develop that contribution further, especially to holistic, worldwide mission.

This was the vision. It had to be translated into reality, through appropriate structures. The earlier steps to develop a new legal and financial structure were dropped, and in their place Interserve (India) was created, designed to express the vision. Several issues had to be faced over the next five years, as described below.

Identity and Function

Interserve (India) was a puzzle to some (and still is today!). If it was the new, Indian expression of Interserve, then should it be saddled with all the baggage of Interserve's past? Would it not be better for it to focus on the recruitment and support of new Indian missionaries (the "home" functions of a mission), leaving the "field" supervision of the existing workers in India (Indian and expatriate) to the international structures of Interserve? Some felt that integration should exist at every level. In practice, there were certain parallel structures, as new patterns were introduced. But by 1992, it was agreed that there should be just one structure, encompassing all the functions of mission. As the Annual Conference and Governing Body affirmed in their vision statement:

> Interserve in India will be our international partnership in cross-cultural mission, serving the church by sending and receiving Partners to proclaim the good news of Jesus Christ by word and deed and to help build His church in India and other regions of the world where Interserve is at work.

> Interserve in India will become Interserve (India), an integrated structure working with the churches and other Christian agencies:

> • To recruit, train, and send Partners to work cross-culturally within India and abroad.

> • To receive Partners from abroad.

- To oversee, facilitate, and develop the ministries of all Partners working in India.

- To develop networks of friends and supporters.

What this statement means in practice is that all functions of Interserve in India are under the Governing Body of the Society, carried out through the staff appointed by it. These functions include the whole range of mission activities, from recruitment to deployment, along with receiving. The focus has been clearly defined in the vision statement in terms of geographical areas and types of ministries.

All these developments have given identity and function to the new body. The Partners feel good about this new identity. But it is still being worked out. For example, in conference we are trying to develop appropriate patterns of worship, planning, cultural and social activity, and recreation!

Leadership

For the first two or three years, the existing leadership (expatriate) carried out all the functions needed to develop the new Society (as Executive Secretary), as well as run the existing programs (as Regional Representative of the international Fellowship). However, these activities were done in close consultation with Partners and with the members of the new Governing Body, and in fact a lot of the work was shared out—for example, writing the new constitution. This helped in the process of integration. Then an Indian Partner was appointed as Executive Secretary—sooner than expected, partly because of government pressure. This was a very healthy development, but it did raise the question of how old and new functions and structures would relate. The issue was resolved with the 1992 vision statement and the integrated structure in which the two main leaders, Executive Secretary and Regional Representative, work in a team, along with others, under the overall leadership of the Executive Secretary.

The Governing Body of the Society is essentially Indian, with a balance of those from inside the Fellowship and those outside

(Partners, both Indian and expatriate). This balance is something to keep working at, as with any organization.

The present leadership combination seems to be healthy,
and we feel that within the team there should be a mixture of
gifts and backgrounds, with the selection of the best available
people, while being sensitive to the right balance of nationalities and cultures.

Another balance to be found is between the autonomy and
"sovereignty" of the Governing Body and its relationship with
the international Fellowship, and particularly the role of the
International Office in India. The International Office is seen
as having a definite role: the international dimension is welcomed and needed.

Finance

Interserve (India) has received generous financial support
from the international Fellowship. This includes underwriting
the support of existing Indian Partners and part of the support
for new ones; subsidy for administration expenses, on a sliding
scale; and a grant for purchase of office space. A formula is
being developed to share expenses, avoiding the extremes of
dependency on one side and of demanding unrealistic "self-
support" on the other. In an international organization, it does
not seem possible to require all the member bodies to contribute equally, when the world's economic order is so manifestly
unequal and exchange rates fluctuate. It may be better to look
for equivalent contributions, though this will require considerable thought and effort to work out.

Personal allowances have also needed attention. Expatriate
and Indian Partners working in India receive different personal
allowances: both the levels and structure are different. This
arises from the earlier historical background, in which most
Indian Partners (and some expatriates) were paid by the institutions in which they worked; newer Indian Partners did not
want to be at a level too different from their counterparts in
other organizations. At that time, it was felt that parity with
other Christian workers was more important than parity with

expatriates. Now with one structure, the issue appears differently, and it has been agreed that there should be parity within Interserve (India). The question is how: which way should allowances be adjusted? The most likely solution is a common level for all allowances in India, somewhere in between the present levels, with separate provision for certain commitments which expatriates may have in their own country. This solution will put Interserve (India's) allowances—and costs—at the higher end of the spectrum of Indian missions, but this arrangement seems appropriate for the professionals whom the mission is largely aiming to recruit.

As new Indian Partners are coming in, new sources of financial support are being found in India. These include the usual sources through churches and friends, but also less traditional channels, such as pensions, partial or full support from employment, grants, and investment from Non-Resident Indians (NRIs) dispersed abroad. Like other missions, Interserve (India) is actively developing links with NRIs—another dimension to worldwide partnership in mission.

Partnership With Other Indian Missions

Partnership with other Indian missions had been a distinctive of Interserve in the past, as already noted, and it is intended that it should continue. But the relationships need to be worked out afresh, as the partnership is not just between the Indian mission and the international body, as before, but with the international body represented by its Indian constituent, which is not just a branch office. The new patterns and channels of communication are still being worked out, but the intention is to continue to work in partnership, both within India and internationally. The Indian Evangelical Mission continues to second to Interserve its missionaries working abroad in an Interserve (India) location. Within India, Interserve (India) has consciously sought to focus its ministry in distinctive ways, so as to avoid unnecessary duplication. All the missions have recognized the freedom and responsibility of others to respond to God's call, while working in harmony and cooperation as much as possible.

Conclusion

The last seven years have seen a new, unexpected phase in the development of partnership for Interserve, particularly in India. Reflections on this experience include:

1. The new pattern was developed for a purpose, to meet new needs and goals in mission. Partnership is not for its own sake, but for partnership in mission.

2. The new pattern was partly developed in response to pressures from outside. However, the response sought to be creative, discerning God's will in the changing situation.

3. What has emerged is something new. Interserve (India) does not look the same as other missionary societies, though it is by no means unique. (IEM, for example, combines both sending and receiving and now has some workers coming from abroad.) It does not even look the same as its original planners expected! It was important that as the new structures were being developed, the focus for ministry was also being reshaped. The new structures were not just for their own sake, but for creative new goals in mission. The link with NRIs was another unexpected new development.

4. What is common with the earlier phase of partnership is the principle of mutual respect and equality, working together to achieve common goals in mission, and being willing to take the time and effort for sharing, listening, and communicating.

5. This is certainly only one model of partnership, but it may prove to be a paradigm for mission in the '90s, where the whole world has become both "field" and "sending country." Complex models, with rich, intertwining relationships, are likely to become more common. What is important is that they develop creative, new patterns for doing new things. (For example, we need to develop ways of being international without necessarily being Western. We still assume that anything which is not "national" or "indigenous" is "Western"—but that need not be the case. However, we will have to demonstrate these alternatives, rather than just talk about them!)

Born in Pakistan, Jim Tebbe was the son of Presbyterian missionaries. From 1977 to 1986, he served in Pakistan and Bangladesh with Interserve. In 1986 he became Area Director West for Interserve and in 1992 Executive Director based in Cyprus. He is married and has four children.

12

Internationalizing Agency Membership as a Model of Partnership

Ronald Wiebe

Meno and Leonila Belen, a godly Filipino couple experienced in Christian service, were convinced that God wanted them in cross-cultural ministry in South America. Their attempt to go with their own denominational mission board was unsuccessful. So they contacted the Philippines Mission Association (PMA). Since the PMA and SIM have a partner mission agreement, the Belens were put in touch with SIM's recently appointed Singaporean Director. Within a short time, the Belens were granted dual membership by PMA and SIM and had been appointed by SIM to a church-planting ministry in Paraguay.

Before they could leave for Paraguay with their four children, they had to wait upon God for His supply of a support team. God provided pastoral/furlough care through the PMA and Filipino churches and monthly financial support through Chinese churches in Indonesia.

The Belens were the first SIMers to locate in Villarrica, a town in southeast Paraguay. Two weeks after settling in Villarrica, the Belens entertained guests, including Dr. Ian Hay, SIM's General Director, and his wife. They prepared a special meal for the occasion and invited their new Paraguayan friends. To the Hays' great surprise, no less than 64 Villarricans showed up. What a beginning for this gregarious, gifted couple!

The Belens arrived this month in Manila for furlough. During their first term, they produced weekly radio Bible studies which covered Villarrica and several surrounding communities. They planted a fledgling church, baptizing 40 new converts. Meno also served as Ministry Coordinator for the area, which gave him oversight for SIMers from Korea, South Africa, and the United States.

This brief comment on the Belens serves to highlight a notable characteristic of SIM: it is and always has been an international mission agency.

SIM's Process of Internationalization

Among the three cofounders of SIM were an American and two Canadians, one born in Scotland and the other in England. On their initial trip to the Sudan in 1893, very little help came from North America. Rather, the encouragement came from the United Kingdom, which they visited en route. God gave them two recruits and provided large gifts for their fares during this brief stopover.

By the year 1927, SIM Councils and constituencies had been formed in Australia, Canada, New Zealand, the United Kingdom, and the United States. Immediately following World War II, SIM entered into a partner agreement with the Deutsche Missions-Gemeinschaf, and in the early 1950s also opened its Lausanne office. These later two initiatives increased SIM's internationalness from a strictly Anglophone membership to also include German and French-speaking Europeans.

Another very significant year in SIM's international development was 1977. The first Asian couple joined the Mission through its Australian office. Subsequently SIM's East Asia office was established in Singapore, and presently 62 Asians are members of SIM.

During the years 1982 and 1989, SIM's internationalness was further enhanced through mergers with the Andes Evangelical Mission (AEM) and the International Christian Fellowship (ICF). The AEM had worked in South America for most of this century, and ICF had done the same, ministering in seven countries of Asia.

Since Anglophones, Francophones, Germanics, and Asians have been mentioned as composing SIM's membership, someone may rightly query, "Are Africans and Latin Americans also free to join SIM?" The answer is an unequivocal "yes." But since these two major regions of the world have constituted the principal locations of SIM's church-planting ministry, primary consideration is always given to the national church with its development and leadership needs.

Owing to a climate of openness and the conscious decision to be multinational, SIM has grown to be a truly international mission. In this writer's view, the two factors which contributed most significantly in developing SIM's international character are that it is interdenominational, and it employs a pooling system for financial support of all its missionaries.

In the early days, Dr. Rowland Bingham, SIM's first General Director, thought of making the Mission a part of his own Canadian Baptist denomination. Through experience and prayer, however, God led Dr. Bingham to form an interdenominational mission which he described succinctly:

> As a Mission, we have been insistent that every candidate shall be, without question, loyal to the fundamentals of the faith, and the great basic doctrines of the Scripture, and God has given us from almost every evangelical denomination men and women who have come together for one common task—the giving of the gospel to every soul in the Sudan.*

---

* Bingham, R. V. (1943). *Seven seven of years and a jubilee* (p. 113). Toronto: Evangelical Publishers.

Bingham also outlined the rationale for his action:

The problem of this basis of Church fellowship is growing more complex every year, and we question whether it will be greatly relieved by the organic unions everywhere proposed. The perpendicular lines which divide the different denominations are, on their own confession, growing more and more unsatisfactory, first because of their exclusions, for in whatever ecclesiastical party one finds himself placed, he is blind who does not recognize that outside it are some of the best saints that God and grace have made and to whom every yearning of Christian love draws one: unsatisfactory also because of its inclusion, for within each separate pale there has crept worldliness and unbelief, corruption in doctrine or departure in faith, so that to the spiritual mind, many and sad are the hindrances to fellowship within this restricted area.

What is to be done? Withdrawal and separation have been tried in order to constitute an ideal body, to end in the creation of yet one more sect, more sectarian than the body from which it has withdrawn. More and more it is being recognized that the lines of fellowship must be drawn horizontally, and that its sweetness will be measured by the plane of our fellowship with our risen Lord—fellowship dependent, not upon knowledge or assenting to common truths, but to "walking in the truth."*

The pooling of support funds is the second key which enables SIM to be international in character. The *SIM Manual* explains the pooling system:

All support funds received are pooled. Each missionary's salary allowance and amenities will be based on the concept of equal earning power from home countries and equal purchasing power at the current location, regard-

---

* Bingham, R. V. (1943). *Seven seven of years and a jubilee* (pp. 110-111). Toronto: Evangelical Publishers.

less of support received, home country, or assignment. All members must participate fully in the support pool, both providing income and receiving benefits.*

The Belen family illustrates how the pooling system works. Having raised the 61 percent support required of SIMers from the Philippines (the SIM uses its United States support requirement as the norm [100 percent] for calculating all other SIM countries' support requirement levels; based on equal earning power calculations, SIMers from the Philippines are presently required to raise 61 percent), they went to Paraguay. They have enjoyed all the same benefits as every other SIMer regardless of geographical location, including a monthly salary of equal purchasing power.

In the providence of God, Bingham's deliberate decision to make SIM interdenominational, and the subsequent policy of pooling financial support funds, have resulted in people joining the Mission from more than 70 denominational backgrounds and from 34 countries of the world.

Advantages of Internationalness

While internationalness brings certain tensions into the SIM, the resultant advantages far outweigh the problems.

Through ongoing orientation and experience, SIM members discover several facts related to the multicultural nature of the Mission:

- It is an expression of the body of Christ.

- It enhances the planting of culturally appropriate churches.

- It enriches personal growth through transcending one's own nationality and culture.

- It provides checks and balances of national tendencies.

---

* *SIM manual* (1991 ed.) (p. 4-4).

SIM also believes and teaches that internationalness enhances a missionary's ability to do the following:

- Understand and appreciate one's own culture.

- Understand and appreciate a fellow worker's culture.

- Understand one's own theology and ecclesiology.

- Understand a fellow worker's theology and ecclesiology.

- Appreciate the primacy of one's citizenship in heaven.

- Consider others better than oneself.

Fully appreciating these positive implications of SIM's internationalness, Dr. Ian Hay makes the observation:

> Most international missions are really confederations of various nationalities, each segregated to its own area of work. SIM seeks to integrate all nationalities into a common work force. We have Asians, Europeans, North Americans, and Australasians working together in their assignments.*

SIM's international makeup has also provided flexibility in developing partner agreements with other missions. This ability has been especially helpful in bringing German and Asian missionaries into world evangelization through SIM. The Mission has partner agreements with nine sister missions in those two areas of the world.

Perhaps one of the greatest advantages of SIM's international philosophy is the present opportunity to partner with its own related churches. The Mission's stated purpose is, "To glorify God by evangelizing the unreached and ministering to human need, discipling believers into churches equipped to fulfill Christ's Commission." The cycle is only completed when the churches planted by SIM become planters of other churches.

---

* Hay, I. M. (1988). *Foundations: Scriptural principles undergirding SIM* (pp. 35-36). Canada: SIM.

The SIM-related Evangelical Churches of West Africa in Nigeria have been sending out their own missionaries for years, and they now number 900. Recently plans have been laid for an Evangelical Missionary Society (ECWA Missions Department) couple to join an SIM ethnic focus team in Chicago for a ministry to Muslims.

Evangel Fellowship, an association of SIM-related churches, was formed in 1981. Its purpose is "to provide SIM-related churches throughout the world with a channel for mutual communication, communion, sharing of resources, and edification to the glory of God, and the fulfillment of the Great Commission of Jesus Christ." Evangel Fellowship currently represents over 8,000 congregations in eight countries, with an estimated 3 million members and adherents. During Evangel's December 1990 meeting, Rev. Panya Baba, President of ECWA's 3,000 churches, challenged Evangel delegates to awaken to their responsibility for cross-cultural evangelism. He went so far as to call for a common strategy and a unified missionary movement. After reminding delegates of the debt of the gospel which each church owes to the unreached within and without the borders of its country, he said:

God has a specific role for His church everywhere in the world. What one church somewhere might not be able to do, another might. For example, some of the unreached ethnic groups in Europe may be better reached by missionaries from Asia and Latin America.

Perhaps it is time now for all of us in every continent to look into how we can set up a real mission force together. We need to come up with a strategy on how to mobilize our churches for foreign missions and send more cross-cultural missionaries to unreached people in Muslim countries in Africa and the Middle East. I believe that if we cooperate together, such cross-cultural missionaries can be found.

I think the time has come for all SIM-related churches to wake up! I think we have been going too slowly. We have been sleeping. The opportunity is vast before us.

This is the right time to lift up our eyes and see the harvest that is due, especially in the regions beyond.*

SIM is delighted with such vision and ready to partner with its related churches as God leads the way.

Tensions Created by Internationalness

The diversity of cultures within SIM membership often produces tension, especially for newcomers. A frequently expressed sentiment sounds something like this: "I expected to experience culture shock in the new country to which I was assigned, and I did. But that shock was not half as bad as the shock I experienced with the SIM culture."

English is the language used worldwide in SIM communications. It places an extra language-learning burden, especially on many Asian SIMers who must study English before taking up their field assignment. Then, upon arrival at their ministry location, they often have to learn both a trade language and a tribal language. Undertaking the study of three different languages in the course of five years may not be recommended by the experts. And it has been known to be counterproductive.

At times, some members of SIM become concerned over the financial pooling policy of the Mission. Such concern is understandable and legitimate, calling for constant monitoring of the practical implications of the policy.

These and other tensions are kept in balance by the realization that God is allowing SIM to serve as a channel of His resources, both human and financial, in an experience of international interdependence in fulfilling Christ's Commission.

---

* Baba, P. (1991, March). Panya Baba challenges delegates to strategize for world evangelism. *Evangel Fellowship Newsletter.*

Born in the USA, Ron Wiebe served as a missionary in Bolivia for 31 years. As General Director of the Andes Evangelical Mission, he was involved in bringing about the merger of AEM with SIM in 1982. Today he serves as Deputy General Director of SIM with international offices located in Charlotte, North Carolina.

13

Tensions in an International Mission*

Brian Butler

With nearly 2,000 missionaries from over 30 countries, SIM International has plenty of opportunities to grapple with tensions in an international mission. Predominantly Western for many years, SIM has more recently received an influx of many others, especially Asians. On the whole, the mission believes that despite the tensions it brings, internationalization has been an enriching and strengthening factor in mission life.

Tensions are inevitable in any organization, and they can be destructive. The fighting in the former Yugoslavia, as well as conflicts in some African countries, shows that cultural and ethnic differences are an incredibly destructive force. Although the church is a divine institution, it's no surprise to find strife, division, and tension among its members. Likewise, the Apostle Paul's mission teams faced strong tensions, and one team split.

---

* Butler, B. (1993, October). Tensions in an international mission. *Evangelical Missions Quarterly*, 412-418. Reprinted by permission of Evangelical Missions Quarterly, Box 794, Wheaton, IL 60189.

International mission agencies are vulnerable to tensions from a number of different sources. Even something as innocuous as introducing a guest speaker can stir up trouble. For example, Europeans and Australians are sometimes embarrassed by American introductions that emphasize the speaker's degrees, qualifications, and offices held. A theological college principal in England may not even have an earned doctorate. When asked what they find most difficult to understand about Americans, Australians sometimes reply, "Their obsession with making a good impression." If such seemingly insignificant things bring trouble, it's hardly surprising that the going gets tougher when the water gets deeper.

Theological Convictions

Apart from the usual theological differences among any group of evangelicals, an international mission is likely to reflect quite different church backgrounds, with some Europeans coming from state churches and some Americans from independent churches.

Members will also differ over charismatic issues, depending on their previous exposure, or lack of it, to charismatic worship styles. Sometimes these differences reflect cultural attitudes. People of certain nationalities find it hard to live with ambiguity, while those from other countries find it easier to live with gray areas. One international mission has put all "card-carrying charismatic" members on one field. That may solve one problem, but it hardly reflects the unity of the body of Christ.

Differences over eschatology frequently boil to the surface, as do disputes about attitudes toward the World Council of Churches, the Roman Catholic Church, and cooperation with non-evangelicals. While these may appear to be non-issues to some members, there are ominous signs of differences over bedrock mission theology: the modifications of traditional evangelical positions on eternal punishment and the lostness of those who have not heard the gospel.

Language and Culture

If English is the *lingua franca* of the mission, does this mean that prayer meetings in Latin America and Francophone Africa must be held in English rather than Spanish or French? It may depend on whether Americans are in the majority. Francophones find this especially irksome. As one mission leader commented, "The use of English in Spanish and French cultures for meetings where everybody speaks Spanish or French is nothing more than cultural imperialism of the English-speaking world."

Europeans who are used to just one Sunday worship service may have a different attitude toward Sunday than other missionaries do. How far is Sunday observance cultural? Should national holidays be the time for missionaries from that country to get together, to the exclusion of others?

Humor and jokes are a notorious minefield for misunderstanding. "At those very points that the American expects seriousness and total attention to the task at hand, the Australian leans back and tosses off a clever quip," says G. W. Renick in his book, *Australians and North Americans*.

Leadership Styles

This is not simply an international issue, although with the influx of Asians into Western missions new leadership patterns are likely to emerge. Koreans tend to be strong top-down leaders, which may prove to be a problem when they move into leadership. Other Asians, such as the Chinese, are more consensus oriented in making decisions. Australians have strongly anti-authoritarian strands in their culture: e.g., the "tall poppy syndrome" (cut leaders down to size if they try to throw their weight around).

Generation Gap

Not strictly international, the generation gap does become a cause of tension. The mission population often reflects pre-World War II thinking, mixed with that of the baby boomers

(1946-1964) and the baby busters (post-1964). It is also worth noting that Asians whose culture reflects deep respect for age may have problems with Western attitudes of young to old.

Attitudes

Here we dip into a huge grab-bag of sore points, including:

- **Money.** Many non-Americans may never have a ministry account, and some may resent the key it provides to a car or children's education.

- **Materialism.** What is a suitable standard of living? Are microwave ovens and freezers appropriate? The problem is compounded when missionaries have different allowances.

- **Lifestyle.** Simple or otherwise?

- **Health.** Shoes or bare feet?

- **Women's roles.** Are they proportionately represented at the mission's highest levels?

- **Children.** Children in Europe are not looked on as their parents' best friends. There is a strong reaction developing against some of the teachings of the American family guru, James Dobson.

- **Education.** Methods, evaluation, roles of teachers and parents. American parents expect to have much more input; others leave more to the teacher.

- **Work.** Goal setting, methods, priorities, appraisals.

What SIM Did

To help alleviate some of these causes of tension, some years ago SIM developed its SIM International Orientation Course (SIMIOC). It was intended for candidates immediately prior to their leaving for the field. It included some culture learning aspects and specific training in appreciating SIM's diversity as people mixed with those from other countries. However, it was disbanded because of logistical complexities and replaced with one for the entire mission family. That, too, floundered because old-timers resented taking more orientation.

Eventually, the course became the SIM International Outlook Course. Some culture-learning segments were drastically
reduced, and other parts were strengthened. A husband and
wife team with previous years of living in Europe, Africa, and
the United States was appointed to hold eight-day seminars
on the various SIM fields.

Generally, this program has been well received. Younger
missionaries have accepted it readily. Some older workers have
asked, "Why didn't the mission have this sort of thing 30 years
ago?" On the other hand, others have resisted the idea and
refused to attend. On the whole, SIMIOC has worked well as a
learning tool to bring to the surface prejudices, hurts, and
misunderstandings that have lain hidden, or have festered for
a long time.

Interestingly, most participants have appreciated the sessions on understanding Asians more than most other things.
Wherever possible, Asians have been included in the course,
both as participants and as leaders.

Of course, it soon emerges that learning styles reflect
culture as much as anything. For example, Americans appreciate the free-for-all of discussion. Throw everything into the
pot and make sure you have your say. The pragmatists are
leery of too much theory, and they do not want too much
lecture material. Europeans, especially Germans, want information from the front, with plenty of content. They suspect any
psychologizing.

The British tend to be overly critical, and this is seen in how
they operate in a seminar. Koreans generally will not speak at
all, unless they are specifically asked to, but this is not true of
Singaporeans and Filipinos. Of course, my generalizations are
themselves somewhat suspect, but they will stand as guide-
posts.

Key Factors

Overcoming these cultural tensions may appear to be an
impossible task, but let me make a few suggestions and
observations. First, although having seminars like SIMIOC

seems like an unaffordable luxury, SIM feels that the considerable cost is worthwhile for the sake of missionary careers and the overall well-being of the mission. SIM has traced missionary attrition to international and relational problems. A full-blown seminar may not be possible, but shorter sessions can be included in annual spiritual life conferences.

While "forbearing one another in love" (Col. 3:13) may be a scriptural injunction, experience suggests it does not happen automatically. Most people are blind to their cultural prejudices, at least until they have in-depth exposure to an alien culture. Even then, though their attitudes may betray it, their minds may not make the connection.

It is necessary to bring these issues to the surface, talk them through, and face them openly. Some people may have imbibed strong prejudices from their parents, or some other environment that they are unaware of.

Missionaries are subject to the media, which are largely responsible for shaping cultural and national stereotypes. The standard images—Americans are immature or childish, the Japanese are devious, the Germans are ruthless—need to be confronted because they subtly damage good relations. Studies show that stereotypes often are based on one extreme example—the loud, brash American tourist, or the large, beer-swilling German—and these stick in our minds when we meet people who don't fit the stereotype.

Of course, international tensions are only one part of interpersonal relations. Younger missionaries often come from problem-filled family backgrounds. Their emotional baggage often carries over into relations with their colleagues from other countries. The danger is that they will have neither the inclination nor the energy to work through their feelings. If not, serious conflicts often develop.

Apart from national and cultural feelings, we also have to deal with those general attitudes that cause problems in the mission family:

• **Intolerance.** The inability to allow for differences of opinion or behavior.

• **Infallibility.** A subtle pride that can as easily surface in agriculture or bookkeeping as in worship and church growth strategies. Those with this attitude "convey the impression that there are only two ways of doing a thing—their way and the wrong way," said J. O. Sanders.

• **Inflexibility.** The inability to adapt, with little to learn and much to criticize in other cultures.

On the other hand, tensions can be considerably reduced as we cultivate such positive attitudes as:

• **Tact.** The ability to place oneself in another person's shoes; a quick and intuitive perception of what is fit and proper and right. Though it often appears to be a natural gift, tact can be learned. Sometimes we are unaware of how tactless we have been unless someone tells us.

• **Courtesy.** A somewhat old-fashioned ideal in the West, but still a dominant feature of Asian life. Basically, it is thoughtfulness and consideration for the other person's well-being, and the desire to please, not in an obsequious way, but with quiet dignity.

• **Humility.** The absence of a sense of superiority. In our SIMIOC seminars, we often say that Philippians 2:3 is our text: "... in humility consider others better than yourselves." Non-Christians can accept the idea of equality, but only by God's grace can Christians esteem others better than themselves.

Very few of us are prepared to admit that another person's values, cultural norms, or attitudes are better than our own. Yet exposure to other cultures should teach us this lesson. Each nationality and culture has strengths and weaknesses. We need to appropriate the strengths and know our own weaknesses. We may believe that "ours is the greatest country in the history of the world," but that is not a helpful attitude to trumpet to the world at large. National pride is valid, but a sense of national superiority in an international mission is not.

On a practical level, whether or not the mission agency wants to develop a seminar like SIMIOC, it can at least ask both old and new missionaries to read about other nationalities and cultures. Generally, new missionaries are well-prepared with anthropological and cross-cultural training with regard to their host countries, but they may be less familiar with the cultures of their fellow missionaries. Therefore, they can benefit from a recommended reading list. These are some of the more popular works:

• *The Europeans.* By Luigi Barzini (Penguin Books, 1984). Immensely readable and informative, with chapters like "The Quarrelsome French," "The Imperturbable British," and "The Mutable Germans." A final chapter on "The Baffling Americans."

• *Mind Your Manners.* By John Mole (London: The Industrial Society, 1990). Written primarily for business people working in Europe, it has excellent material on culture in short chapters on all 12 countries in the European Community, plus chapters on "Americans in Europe" and "Japanese in Europe."

• *Culture Shock.* An excellent series published by Times Books International in Singapore, *Culture Shock* is followed in the various titles by the name of a country: *Culture Shock: France,* or *Culture Shock: Korea.*

From a vast selection of books on American culture, the following may be recommended:

• *The American Character.* By D. W. Brogan (New York: Knopf, 1944). Brogan was an eminent British observer of American history, and his old book is still readable.

• *The American Character: Views of America from The Wall Street Journal.* Edited by Donald Moffitt (New York: Braziller, 1983). Diversity is the hallmark of this book.

• *Talks About America, 1951-1968.* By Alistair Cooke. (Penguin Books, 1981). Listeners to the BBC World Service will need no recommendation to seize anything by the preeminent British interpreter of the American scene to non-Americans.

• A truly indispensable book for understanding missionary relationships is *Florence Allshorn,* by J. H. Oldham (SCM Press, 1951). Oldham describes her experiences in Uganda and how she overcame some bitter conflicts. After one bruising encounter with a fellow missionary, an African said to her, "I have been on this station for 15 years, and I have seen you come out, all of you saying you have brought to us a Saviour, but I have never seen this situation (i.e., the inability of missionaries to live in harmony) saved yet." For a whole year she read 1 Corinthians 13 and wrestled and prayed until that situation was saved. Florence went on to found a community, St. Julian's, where the principles she had learned could be exemplified and imparted to others. Much of her teaching is found in this biography.

Creative Tension

Tensions are inevitable because personal relationships lie at the heart of any organization. Relationships between people of different nationalities within a mission are just one dimension of such tension. Left unchecked, or ignored, problems will fester and become a hindrance to spiritual vitality and to the work. However, the attitudes that underlie cultural insensitivity and relational problems are identifiable and curable.

Despite the inherent problems in international missions, their diversity can also be a strength. For one thing, a multicultural mission can incarnate the first principle of the church, which is that in the body of Christ "there is no difference between Jew and Greek, between slaves and freemen, between men and women; you are all one in union with Christ Jesus" (Gal. 3:28, GNB).

As a result, churches planted on this basis are more likely to express this biblical ideal and to be culturally relevant. We can avoid the incongruity of some denominational labels with which some new churches are burdened. As Stephen Neill once said, "Converts are imitative." Often they tend to copy those appurtenances of their mentors, such as dog collars and incense, rather than the deeper fundamentals.

"In comparatively few areas have missionaries deliberately tried to Westernize their converts: but converts are imitative, and have always been inclined to make the same mistakes as their Western friends, imagining that things which are merely Western trappings ought to be accepted by the new Christians as evidences of the sincerity of their faith" (Stephen Neill, *Colonialism and Christian Mission*, p. 416).

Coming from different cultures preserves us from identifying our cultural mores with the gospel, since our assumptions along these lines are continually being challenged by our fellow workers. This is not to say that we can ever plant an a-cultural church, but a church planted by Aussies, Germans, Canadians, and Asians is likely to be multicultural from the start, even if it has a baptism of fire before a baptism in water takes place.

People whose background, upbringing, education, and mission orientation have been monocultural will have little awareness of how these affect their assumptions, attitudes, work patterns, and leadership. They may serve their whole career believing them to be normative. This is not to say that they cannot be successful, but they will leave a difficult legacy for their converts to cope with.

More and more missionaries are working with national churches already in place. They will still have problems adjusting to their fellow workers from different countries, but they won't have to wrestle with what kind of church to plant.

Time and energy spent in planning and implementing training to defuse tensions in international missions will be amply rewarded by stronger, more culturally sensitive, and probably humbler workers.

Brian Butler, a native of England and former missionary to Nigeria, now serves with the International Department of SIM. He and his wife Maureen hold seminars in relationships among SIM missionaries. He is a graduate of London University and Eastern Baptist Seminary, Philadelphia, Pennsylvania. We have included this article in our book because of Butler's incisive and realistic treatment of the subject.

14

The Benefits and Problems of Internationalizing Missions

From the perspective of an Asian
working in a predominantly Western agency

Joshua K. Ogawa
Japan Evangelical Association

Two questions were often asked me when I accepted God's call to foreign missions in 1969, until I took up a new denominational responsibility back in Japan in 1990:

• "Why do you have to go overseas? Japan is still a mission field where over 98 percent of the population are non-Christians."

• "Why do you belong to a Western-oriented mission? There are quite a number of indigenous missionary societies in Japan."

These questions may not be fully answered during my earthly life. But the past 17 years of my missionary service and the present ministry based in Japan have helped me to understand some of the reasons God called me to foreign missions for the significant period of 17 years with a predominantly Western mission operating in Asia.

173

The benefits of international missionary service have been numerous in terms of cross-cultural fellowship and ministries. At the same time, however, I had to face problems and difficulties concerning my missionary identity, whether cultural or spiritual.

An Asian Perspective in a Western Mission

For the first 100 years of its existence, OMF (the former China Inland Mission) had only Western members. But since 1965, some Asians were invited as fellow members. According to the statistics of January 1988, out of 983 members, 73 were Asians including some from the West. The number of Asian missionaries has been steadily increasing. But these Asian members, if understood, accepted, and integrated well into the mission, have within themselves a potential for valuable contributions to the mission. I once presented at a directors' conference an Asian perspective on some of the benefits and problems of internationalizing missions.* Here is a summary of some of my reflections:

First, Asian members are often regarded as representatives of their home churches in Asia. This understanding may be true with the Western counterparts, but it is more so with the Asians because of their corporate nature of society. Most Asian members are pioneer missionaries with much expectation from their churches at home.

This strong sense of "groupism" or corporateness of Asians could be in great contrast with the individualism with which much of the Western thinking has been dominated, even in missions. While an Asian missionary's loyalty to his or her home church is something to be assumed throughout the missionary life, not a few Western missionaries have been called in isolation and go on their own way, thus owing no

---

* Ogawa, J. K. (1983). *Asian missionaries in the OMF.* Paper presented at the Overseas Council Meeting of Overseas Missionary Fellowship.

serious allegiance to their home church. This difference takes another shape when a missionary arrives on the field. Generally speaking, an Asian would try to integrate himself or herself into some of the existing churches, but Westerners might examine whether the local churches fit their idea of church or not, and if not, they can be easily bypassed.

Corporateness and individualism should be balanced in missions, because the gospel of the Triune God and the church as the family of God has both aspects. Internationalizing missions is one key to maintain the balance in the midst of these conflicting approaches. But if the Western mission insists on operating in its own way, it often is detrimental to its Asian members and their churches.

Second, Asian missionaries have a potential to bring about significant changes in the mission society leading towards a richer fellowship in the Lord, but only if Asian members are well integrated into the fellowship. The Lord has blessed the Asian churches with many cultural and spiritual gifts. Their missionaries can share these gifts with their Western counterparts. Asians are still very much people oriented. What matters is relationships, and moreover, harmonious relationships. Relationships often count more than programs or their achievement. The Asian emphasis on the maintenance of balance and harmony in relationships can be a great contribution to Western goal setting, projects, and processes which are centered around success and achievement. Though there is a biblical emphasis on strategies and plans in mission, there is a greater biblical truth of harmonious relationship in mission, for mission is, after all, the restoration and reconciliation of relationships in the Lord Jesus Christ.

But in reality, lack of cross-cultural perspective in an international mission causes racial superiority or inferiority among its members. In order to overcome this danger, there must be some mediators from the majority group who have enough experience in Asia and have a real understanding of Asians. At the same time, there must be a willingness on the part of Asians to learn about Western culture and church backgrounds.

Third, if Asian members are well integrated, they can be the bridge to the mission's deeper involvement in Asian missions. Asian missionaries have their own mission perspectives, because they have already experienced and observed the work of many of the Western missionaries in their home countries, with all their successes and failures.

Westerners have been much better trained in their abstract, logical, analytical, and critical way of thinking. As a result, Western missionaries seek to maintain clearly defined doctrinal statements wherever they go. They seem to reflect the Greek and New Testament approach. As an extreme example, some Western missionaries think that what qualifies the right teacher most is full intellectual information on the subject.

Asians, on the other hand, normally expect others to live out what is known intellectually. Quantity and content of intellectual knowledge are less respected than their visible practice. Asians think more concretely and seek to convey their messages more through their lives than through doctrinal teachings. Thus, according to my observation, Asian missionaries can recover Old Testament perspectives on God's mission.

Some of the cultural practices of Asians, therefore, can contribute to more effective evangelism and pastoral care in Asian mission fields. There are things in Asian missions that Asian missionaries can see very clearly, which Western counterparts cannot see. Sometimes the reverse may also be true. Both groups have their problems and need to learn from each other. What is desired is a mutual understanding and a genuine cooperation between Western and Asian members.

Fourth, although Asia is a vast and needy mission field, Asian missionaries should not be confined only to Asia but should be set free for world mission. Usually Western missionaries emphasize missions during their deputation at home, but when they return to their work in the Asian field, they do not share this vision as they should. In other words, they do not want to lose their national Christians and money for other works in other areas. Some Asian missionaries have been aware of this blind spot and are freshly challenging Asian Christians and churches for world mission.

In a Western-oriented mission such as OMF, Asian missionaries are often expected to be like the Westerners in thinking and doing things. Westernization of the minority Asians is encouraged and welcomed, because it makes the mission society easier to operate and be in control. There is no question about the necessity of Asians' learning Western cultures. But when it comes to important discussions or decision making regarding missions in Asia, a real understanding and agreement can never be reached by Asians becoming like Westerners. Both parties must aim at maturity in cross-cultural understandings and in spiritual discernment, spending enough time for prayer and waiting. Hasty and careless decisions have always caused mistakes and failures. If the mission will not seek for this maturity and endurance, some conscientious member, whether Asian or Westerner, will choose to leave the mission society.

Christian Spirituality

In today's mission, the spiritual goal of the missionary and the way of carrying out the mission strategy have often been taken for granted. Among so-called evangelical Christians, spiritual development is assumed to come almost automatically as a by-product when a person is saved. It is regarded as a matter of information and cognitive process. I have seen much of this in Western churches and in biblical, theological, and missionary training institutions. This understanding of spirituality has already become widespread in Asia as well.

However, there have been other emphases and understandings of spirituality among Asians and in Asian countries. As we think of the internationalization of missions, we should never forget the different approaches to and expectations of Christian spirituality which are represented by missionaries and their churches.

COMPARISON OF THREE SCHOOLS OF SPIRITUALITY			
	Devotional	**Intellectual**	**Behavioristic**
Significance	Being in God's presence	Knowing about God	Doing things for God
Focus	Christ centered	Holy Spirit centered	God centered
Emphasis	Love of God	Holiness of God	Justice of God
Training Method	Devotion and prayer	Scriptural information	Taking action
Basic Question	Who is the spiritual person?	What is the spiritual person?	What should the spiritual person do?
Approach	Mystic and intuitional	Conceptual and dogmatic	Activist

In the table above, sharp differentiations have been made among the three approaches. However, we need to remember that there are several common factors. These are prayer, Scripture, and Christian service.

As far as my observation goes, missionary movements from the West have tended to define missionary spirituality in terms of either "knowing" or "doing," while in many parts of Asia, for example, the "being" perception of spirituality may predominate. Indeed, any group of people, whether national, ethnic, religious, or social, has its own understanding, expectation, and felt need as to spiritual development. Emphasis on the different aspects of spirituality will certainly vary according to each particular group.

Internationalization of missions will bring forth many benefits both within the mission and in the mission fields, as long as two emphases are made. First, internationalization must aim at a deeper understanding of Christian spirituality. Second, missionaries must be trained to develop and manifest their spirituality in such a way that it can be understood and accepted by the people to whom they seek to present the unique gospel of Jesus Christ.

Missionary Credibility

One of the major crises for Asian missionaries is in regard to their missionary credibility. Some Asian single lady missionaries have shared with me that the nationals look on them as if they were just helpers for the white missionaries. Japanese missionaries in Asia can be viewed as invaders, owing to past history. Internationalization of missions may help missionaries to establish their credibility in a unique way.

For people in Asia in general, the concept of a missionary is still a blond-haired white man or woman, whether from Europe, North America, or some other country. It takes years of patience and waiting until the concept of the Asian missionary is well-formed in the mind of the missionary himself or herself, as well as in the minds of Western missionaries and nationals.

According to Webster's Dictionary, having credibility is "to be worthy of influence, honor, and power based on the trust of others." As the missionary lives among the nationals and brings the gospel to them, his or her credibility can create in the minds and hearts of the people some positive expectation towards the new life in Christ.

Tentatively, I would look at missionary credibility on three levels from my own experience: ascribed credibility, newly recognized credibility, and divine credibility.

Ascribed Credibility

Ascribed credibility comes from a degree of trust in the missionary which already exists in the minds of people in the field, either because of their common cultural aspects or because of their mutual political, economic, and other kinds of national relationships. The source of ascribed credibility can be further traced back to human commonness. Sex, age, family relationship, and occupation are some of the reference points for ascribed credibility. Of course, the degree of credibility based on these matters may vary according to culture and individuality. But, generally speaking, most cultures arbitrarily assign or ascribe credibility concerning any foreigner without reference to innate differences. In other words, ascribed credibility is something that can be predicted before a person goes into a new culture. The missionary must find and redeem this credibility and must be faithful to it for the sake of the ministry of the Word. Positively speaking, international missions can choose to send to the mission field those missionaries who have a greater degree of ascribed credibility. To put it negatively, they can prevent unnecessary ascribed discredit of some missionaries.

It must be remembered, however, that ascribed credibility may not always be the decisive way of bringing the gospel into the hearts of people. The cultural, racial, and national advantages related to ascribed credibility may often cease to work as we aim at reaching the level of spiritual communication on the mission field.

Newly Recognized Credibility

Newly recognized credibility is a kind of achieved credibility which is secured by doing and/or getting things. The missionary's aim should be a deeper cultural understanding of the people, of their thinking, and of their emotional and behavioral patterns, together with good language ability and good stewardship. Above all, in the ministries of evangelism, church planting, social work, etc., the missionary should patiently learn from the nationals and should eventually prove himself or herself to be a trustworthy Christian and a minister of the Word in the host culture.

Perhaps the Asian missionary must aim at achieving his or her recognized credibility more, by the grace of God, in a country where Westerners are more respected and thus predominant in missionary service. If the missionary is working in a hostile country in any sense, the need of this credibility is greater. Again, international missions can help their Asian members to establish their credibility.

Divine Credibility

There is yet another, deeper level of discussion concerning credibility. I call it divine credibility. Not only must the missionary be perceived by the people on the field as credible and trustworthy, but his or her message must also be heard and accepted as credible and trustworthy. This is where the work of the Holy Spirit comes in. The person of Jesus Christ as preached and lived by the missionary becomes real for the gospel hearers, because of the divine credibility given by the Holy Spirit to the missionary and the message. This divine credibility causes in the hearts of the hearers a hunger, longing, and desire for a meeting with the true God in Jesus Christ. In a spiritually hostile situation, as well as in friendly circumstances, human credibility does not help much in bringing people to repentance and faith in Christ. Only divinely given credibility will work. The people must see the image of Christ and smell the fragrance of Him in the missionary's life and service. If necessary, a power encounter needs to be exercised as well. If the Lord wills, the missionary should be willing to go through crises of life for the sake of the gospel, as my family experienced in the riot in Java and the heavenly homecalling of one of our children.*

Missionary Training

Recently there has been a serious concern with quality in education in general and in theological training in particular. As a result, various holistic integrated approaches to ministerial training have been worked out. It has been suggested that the traditional formal education, which very often overemphasizes the academic component of education, should be integrated with the non-formal and informal patterns of training. This is encouraging news for us Asian mission leaders, who

---

* Ogawa, J. K. (1986). *Unlimited purpose: An Asian missionary tells his story* (pp. 2-25). Singapore: Overseas Missionary Fellowship.

have long been waiting for such a change of trend in ministerial training. Missionary training must follow this pattern, too.

But according to my observation, there is always a tendency for any educational institution to remain in or revert to the traditional formal pattern of training. Various reasons can be thought of. Formal education is still much more attractive and acceptable in society because of the professional competence of the instructors and the degrees awarded to the successful students. Moreover, non-formal and informal education are difficult to evaluate and develop. Obviously, more holistic qualifications for the instructors are required, based on their actual experiences of life and field work.

If we pursue excellency in training, however, we have to resist the tendency to become predominantly formal in our educational structures. However difficult, we should be aiming at the right integration of formal, informal, and non-formal training patterns. These patterns, by their nature, must seriously consider contextualization of education.* Asian missionary training is something which cannot be effectively conducted without such contextualization. A number of reasons come to mind:

First, contextualization of education involves making the training sensitive to the specific needs of the trainees in its educational form or to the appropriate ways of undertaking a task in a given cultural context.

Second, contextualization of education must ask whether or not the training is committed to developing the spirit of servanthood, rather than being dominated by racial, educational, financial, or political superiority. It is sad indeed that education has so often been political. It has already been pointed out, for instance, that any education which makes the national Christians more dependent upon foreign personnel,

---

* Conn, H. M., & Rowen, S. F. (1983). *Missions and theological education in world perspective* (pp. 144-145). Farmington, MI: Associates of Urbanus.

money, and materials is a political act, and it never liberates the students.

Contextualization in missionary training in Asia is a good example. For contextualization to occur, organizational structure and its leadership must be firmly rooted in missionary-minded Asian churches and in missions whose work has proved to be relevant and acceptable in Asia. But often local churches have been bypassed, and some ambitious Western missions and/or parachurch organizations have taken advantage of the situation to promote an attractive project.

Third, it is much more desirable in Asian missionary training that the leading full-time teaching and training staff should be those experienced Asian missionaries who are well understood and supported by their home churches in Asia, and whose cross-cultural lives and ministries with their spiritual gifts have proved to be effective in some particular mission field in Asia. In other words, they should have well understood the reality of Asian missionary struggles, the real needs of Asian missionaries, and ways to meet these needs. If there are any difficulties with personnel, we should be prayerfully waiting for the right people to be raised for the ministry and the right time to come. Hasty decisions with an expectation of ex post facto approval will bring an irretrievable result. Both on the board and the staff levels, several Asian countries should be represented. Western missionaries who are willing to take supportive roles will be very much appreciated.

Fourth, as we see the greatest need of church planting and pastoral care in the context of the church in Asia, missionary training in Asia must reflect church-centered training by church-centered instructors through church-centered means. Both on the board and the staff levels, Asians with sufficient church experience are preferable to lead the training program. But somehow this perspective has been blurred by too much emphasis on academic training as something final for mission training.

Fifth, as my last perspective, I would like to refer to a pitfall in mission education in Asia. It is true that much missiological thinking has been developed by Western missionaries and missiologists. As a result, many mission courses are available in the West, and missionaries from the West are able and willing to teach on mission wherever they go. Asian missionaries and national workers should humbly learn from them. But there is a subtle problem, as Jim Pleuddemann points out in *A Call for World Christian Educators*. He says that Western missionaries can hinder the development of Asian Christian leadership by wanting to be in control.*

Martin F. Goldsmith's reflection on church growth in Indonesia focuses on the same point:

> Sadly, the immense growth of the church in Indonesia has attracted a large number of foreign missionaries desiring to jump on the bandwagon of success. The majority of such missionaries refuse to inject their endeavors into the existing Indonesian churches, but rather insist on developing new movements which are often in rivalry with national Christians and therefore push themselves into leadership positions and steal the limelight. The danger is that we may again give the image of foreignness to the Christian church in Indonesia. If we do so, we shall have damaged the Indonesian churches and the long-term prospects for the progress of the gospel of Jesus Christ.**

In internationalizing missions, both Asian and Western missionaries and mission leaders in Asia need to be aware of this danger as we see missionary movements emerging from Asian churches. Internationalization could be a hindrance for contextualization.

Concluding Remark

Internationalizing missions involves us in tremendous tensions, which are caused by cultural differences, conflicting

---

* Pleuddemann, J. (1987). *A call for world Christian educators* (p. 11).

** Goldsmith, M. F. (1983). The Karo Batak. In W. Shenk (Ed.), *Exploring church growth* (p. 41). Grand Rapids: Eerdmans.

family structures and personal value systems and priorities, and different financial and personnel policies. At the same time, today we are living and serving in a very pluralistic society in terms of culture and religion. There is much to be frustrated with, from both inside and outside Christian and missionary circles.

In the midst of this spiritual chaos, we have been called to the task of proclaiming the uniqueness of Christ. Whatever cultural and national background we are from, the foundational principle of our mission is that of love. "If I speak in the tongues of men and of angels... if I have the gift of prophecy and can fathom all mysteries and all knowledge... if I have a faith that can move mountains... if I give all I possess to the poor, and surrender my body to the flames... but have not love, I am nothing... and gain nothing" (1 Cor. 13:1-3). Means of communication, a deep knowledge of the Scriptures and of this world, a strong faith in God, and the spirit of sacrifice are all indispensable to missions. But these spiritual gifts lose their innate effectiveness when they are exercised without Christian love.

How often missionary enterprises have been attempted without seriously examining the basic motive of their leaders and coworkers! The principle of love has been taken for granted. But sooner or later the divine test will come, and the real picture of the work and the workers will be revealed. However difficult and painful the test may be, those who hold firmly to their first love will be able to endure and bear much fruit. Their fruit will never fail because the love in which they are rooted endures forever.

Born in Japan and trained in physics, theology, and missions, Joshua K. Ogawa served as a missionary in Indonesia and in Singapore from 1973 to 1989 with Overseas Missionary Fellowship. He is the founding dean of the Asian Missionary Training Institute (now known as ACTI) in Singapore. Since 1990 he has been the General Secretary of the Evangelical Free Church of Japan. Married, he has two daughters at university and a son 12 years old.

Part Four:
Models of Partnership

15

Partnership in Mission: OMF in a Unique China Partnership

David Pickard

Models in Partnership

CIM/OMF has, throughout its 127 years, worked with different models of cooperative partnership in the task of evangelization, first in China and then in East Asia.

Associate Missions

Early on in China, under Hudson Taylor's leadership, the CIM developed partnerships with other missions. At one point, at least 15 missions worked in association with the China Inland Mission. Under the arrangement as Associates, each mission retained its separate identity and language, working together as a team or group. They would be assigned particular areas for ministry (geographic or a specialized ministry), working within CIM's goals and strategy for the evangelization of China. While some interchange of personnel was possible, it was not common.

The pattern of cooperation and partnership has continued to the present, expressed in Christian ministry.

Mission Partnerships With Western Missions

This refers to joint ventures or projects between Western missions for a variety of tasks. Among many, I would include the following two as representing the tasks of evangelism, church planting, and theological education. The first is called The Karachi Project, formed by Interserve and OMF for evangelism and church planting in Karachi; the second example is the Bangkok Bible College and Bangkok Theological Seminary, founded by OMA and OMF jointly as a higher level Bible college and seminary for training Thai men and women.

Mission Partnerships With the Asian Church

Often, as churches are planted in areas or countries or among people where no churches existed previously, there are new opportunities for evangelism and church planting, through forming partnerships with the church that has been planted. Thus, OMF now works in partnership with churches planted by OMF and now formed into the Evangelical Church Association in Japan, the Association of Churches of Thailand, and the Alliance of Bible Christian Communities of the Philippines in the Philippines.

Mission Partnership With Asian and Western Organizations

Partnerships may be international and cross-cultural in their composition, in which Asian and Western organizations organize together for specific projects.

A good example is the Asian Cross-Cultural Training Institute in Singapore. Founded originally by OMF, the Institute was then reconstituted with seven other Western and Asian organizations to form the Asian Cross-Cultural Training Institute (ACTI). The purpose of ACTI is to train Asian and some Western missionary appointees for cross-cultural service. Thus, by joining together in this way, the needs and experiences of East and West are blended together to more effectively train missionaries for cross-cultural living and ministry.

Mission Partnership With Asian
Parachurch Organizations

A recent example, the "Pledge of Partnership" made by OMF and two Asian parachurch organizations, is developed more fully at the end of this paper.

Internationalization

1965 marked a watershed in the history of OMF, when Asians were accepted as full members. This was a major step forward, as Asian colleagues worked shoulder to shoulder in evangelism and church planting. To facilitate sending Asian missionaries, indigenous sending bases that were both independent and working within OMF's goals and ethos were established in the countries of East Asia.

Principles in Partnerships

While there are many possible combinations of cooperation and many models in partnership, there are some basic principles that are common to all. I would like to suggest four such principles that can contribute to the success of any partnership.

1. Partnerships Are Dynamic, Not Static

Partnerships are always in a process of development. Signing a formal agreement should not be thought of as the end, but rather the beginning of the partnership. Indeed, partnerships may and should grow, as interpersonal relationships develop and as trust among the partners is strengthened. We should recognize that when partnership agreements are made, a process has begun that *may lead to further changes* in the project or to new partnerships.

2. Partnerships Require Integrity

Partners are servants, and partnerships succeed where members *serve*. 1 Corinthians 10:24 is the principle: "Let no one seek his own good but the good of his neighbor." Therefore, partnerships require integrity in respecting the selfhood of other members or partners. The integrity and independence of each partner must be respected, along with the unique gift and contribution each one makes. This means that while there may be different methods of working among member partners, these differences must be acknowledged, and any attempt to force all parties into a common mold must be stoutly resisted.

Furthermore, there must be integrity of motivation in joining a partnership. This tackles the question: Why has this partnership been entered into? What is the motive behind the agreement? Is the partnership brought about because it is right for the sake of the kingdom or because it is in vogue and it appeals? Are we doing it for God or for our own organization's good or reputation?

Finally, integrity and trust must exist among members. Partnerships require maximum, not minimum mutual acceptance of each other, and this means there should be no hidden agendas among the partners.

3. Partnerships Require Long-Term Thinking

It takes time to build relationships among partners. It takes time to understand one another's perspectives. Partnerships that succeed often have a long lead time to build up relationships between the partners, before finalizing and formalizing the partnership.

It takes time to work through the implications of partnerships and to adjust to the increased commitment of time and energy expected of member partners.

Partnerships also have long-term implications. Though it is true that some partnerships can be formed for a specific project and then be disbanded, most partnerships, by the nature of the work we are called to do, require a long-term commitment. There must be a willingness from the beginning to work for the long term rather than for short-term results.

4. Partnerships Require Clarity

Clarity of Purpose

From the very beginning, in forming a partnership, all parties must be quite clear about the purpose(s) for which the partnership is being formed. Basic questions include the following: What is/are the goal(s) to be achieved? What contribution to that goal(s) or objective(s) is each partner expected to make to the partnership? These questions must be asked, clarified, and hammered out to the satisfaction and agreement of all. Clear agreement from the beginning will help to avoid disappointments and unrealized expectations later.

Clarity in Communication

Partnerships require careful and clear communication between partners. Differences in background, viewpoint, values, and methodology all exist. It is all too easy to make unfounded assumptions about the views, feelings, and assumptions of another partner. Unless there is clear communication, misunderstandings and unfulfilled expectations can cause the partnership to founder. Clarity in communication requires regular meetings to monitor, review, and evaluate the partnership and identify and deal with potential stress points.

New Model in Partnership:
Hong Kong, 1992

In June 1992, a new model for partnership for ministry to the Chinese was established. Three organizations—Overseas Missionary Fellowship, Far East Broadcasting Company Limited, and Christian Communications International—signed a "Pledge of Partnership" to work together in a new model of integrated ministry in Chinese ministries (see pages 194-195).

The three organizations had, in the last decade, already worked informally together in ministry to the Chinese, through radio, literature, and church-related ministries. Now in 1992, with a new era of strategic opportunity in Chinese ministries opening up, the three agencies saw the need to work more effectively together and to enhance the task. Therefore, after careful and prayerful discussions, the three organizations pledged themselves to work in partnership expressed in:

- Strategic planning.
- Stewardship of resources.
- Service in the areas of research, radio, literature and other media, and church-related and other ministries.

This partnership commits the partners to be willing to plan and strategize together and to steward resources, including sharing research facilities and information as well as personnel.

This Pledge of Partnership embodies the principles on which successful partnerships are built. First, it is recognized that the Pledge is but a beginning for the three organizations to build on as the ministry opportunities widen and the degree of cooperation deepens.

Second, it is recognized by member partners that each brings a specific and particular ministry contribution. When each ministry is put in combination with the others, the total ministry is much greater than the sum of the parts. Each member has a unique contribution that complements rather than competes with the others.

Third, integrity has been established. This is because this partnership has been built on the basis of long-term relationships built up by thinking and working together. The trust between members allows each to develop its own contribution without fear or threat from the others.

Fourth, because of close proximity working together in Hong Kong, good face-to-face communication on a regular basis is possible.

Partnership agreements require change by those who wish to make them. They require changes in attitudes and changes in relationships. Someone wisely has said that people do not fear change, but only loss. True partnerships, however, do not take away; they add to and strengthen the hands of member partners. I believe this Pledge of Partnership, flowing from a common goal to glorify God by the urgent evangelization of Chinese millions, and demonstrating a unity for which Jesus Christ prayed (John 17:23), is a model which God can use for His glory and the edification of His people.

David Pickard was born in the UK and served with OMF in Thailand from 1970 to 1984 as Hospital Administrator and Area Director. In 1984, he moved to OMF's International Headquarters in Singapore as Director for Overseas Ministries, and in 1991 he became the eighth General Director of CIM/OMF. Married, he has three children, two at university and one recently graduated.

Pledge of Partnership

Our common goal is to glorify God by the urgent evangelization of China's millions, to the end that Christ's kingdom may come.

The risen Lord called us into being and commissioned us for this sacred task at moments of strategic opportunity.

In 1865, in response to the challenge of unreached peoples in inland China, the China Inland Mission/Overseas Missionary Fellowship was brought into being.

In 1946, in response to the challenge of radio as an innovative tool in the evangelization of China, Far East Broadcasting Company was brought into being.

In 1971, in response to the challenge for Chinese leadership in Christian literature and education, Christian Communications Limited was brought into being through a merger of Christian Witness Press and China Sunday School Association, Hong Kong.

We rejoice that during the past decades of service, the Lord enabled us to enjoy a measure of cooperation.

Now, in 1992, a new era of strategic opportunity in Chinese ministries is before us. We are delighted to see an ever-widening open door. This calls for more effective stewardship of our resources. We are convinced, therefore, that the time has come to establish a new model of integrated ministry which will also serve as a testimony of our unity in Christ.

Our Lord prayed that His disciples might be brought to complete unity to let the world know that the Father had sent Him (John 17:23). The Apostle Paul also exhorts us to make every effort to keep the unity of the Spirit through the bond of peace, that the whole body, being joined and held together, may grow, building itself up in love as each part does its work (Eph. 4:3, 16).

Pledge of Partnership (cont.)

To this end, we pledge ourselves to work together in partner-ship in Chinese ministries expressed in:

A. Strategic planning,

B. Stewardship of resources, and

C. Service in the areas of

- Research

- Radio

- Literature and other media

- Church-related and other ministries.

We, the undersigned, as representatives of our respective organizations, on this the eleventh day of June, nineteen hundred and ninety-two, hereby wholeheartedly endorse and pledge our partnership.

Christian Communications International

Far East Broadcasting Company Limited

Overseas Missionary Fellowship

16

COMIBAM: Three Interdependent Partnerships in Latin America

Rodolfo "Rudy" Girón

COMIBAM International is a movement which represents the emerging missionary endeavor in Latin America and Hispanic North America. COMIBAM is also functioning as a clearinghouse for different national missionary movements on the continent.

There are seven areas that COMIBAM is developing as its main agenda:

- *Intercession*, developing prayer cell groups for missions.

- *Information*, producing the bulletin *Luz para las Naciones*.

- *Instruction*, involving missionary training and the development of missionary literature in the Spanish language.

- *Involvement*, creating missionary awareness among the local churches in Latin America by developing local, denominational, national, and international plans for adopting unreached people groups.

- *Infrastructure*, developing missionary agencies to recruit, equip, and send missionaries.

197

- **Investigation**, focusing on research and information.

- **Inspiration**, developing significant events such as congresses, conferences, and consultations, which will motivate and inspire people to become committed to world missions.

In some of the areas mentioned above, COMIBAM has been developing significant partnerships in order to accomplish the goals proposed. Before we examine some of those partnerships, it is necessary to make some clarifying statements regarding our understanding and ownership of the idea of partnership.

Cultural Presuppositions

It is remarkable that the English term "partnership" is foreign to the Spanish language. So is the meaning that Anglo-speaking people attach to it. The closest word in Spanish is *socio*, meaning "business co-owners." This example stands as a reminder of the difficulties we face, for even language creates obstacles to be overcome in order to come to a clear understanding between two parties.

Other elements to overcome are some attitudes shown in the relationship between missions in the North and churches in the South. Almost as a rule, in partnerships between a Latin American and a North American organization in which financial help is involved, the Latin fears the traditionally applied "Golden Rule" ("the one who owns the gold sets the rule"). Therefore, trust and very close and clear relationships need to be developed.

Many cultural barriers have to be overcome, such as the North American concern over accountability. Among many Latins, this issue has the suspicion of being a means of controlling the agenda of an organization. Therefore, it must be treated with much sensitivity.

It is also necessary to develop a very open and clear personal communication, so that any aspect that can damage the relationship of the parties involved in the partnership can be discussed. Both organizations must be open to being criticized and to doing the proper, permissible changes in order to keep the relationship alive.

Background

In 1991, COMIBAM as a movement proposed a potential partnership to five North American organizations (OC International; Latin American Mission; Church of God (Cleveland), World Missions Department; Mission to the World; and Partners International), for the purpose of gaining support morally and financially. COMIBAM had already entered into partnership with the WEF Missions Commission.

The fact is that COMIBAM, with its own defined agenda, needs the financial support of other groups in order to develop its agenda. The proposal that was made was aimed at forming a consortium of North American mission agencies to support the work of COMIBAM. These organizations know the work of COMIBAM, and they also know that this movement has the support of a large constituency of believers in Latin America. As a result of that initial dialogue, three types of partnership have emerged.

Types of Partnership

1. Sharing Personnel With a Denomination

Description

The Church of God (Cleveland), a Pentecostal denomination, through a special decision of its missions board, agreed to second one of its ordained ministers to work full time as president of COMIBAM International. This decision is remarkable, because very rarely an Anglo denomination missionary board backs up an Hispanic minister to work in a parachurch organization.

Terms of the Partnership

The Church of God World Missions Department will support the missionary financially. This means that through the common method of deputation, this missionary has to come to the American and Hispanic churches of the USA to raise his financial support.

The missionary will be accountable for his ministry as president of COMIBAM to the Board of Directors of COMIBAM. As an ordained minister of the denomination, the missionary must also be accountable to the local leaders of the denomination, especially for his ministerial activities. This requires a monthly report of his ministerial activities.

Advantages of the Partnership

Without losing his denominational ties (crucial to sustain a recognized ministry among his fellow national brethren), the missionary is allowed to work with a parachurch interdenominational entity such as COMIBAM.

Problems

Being a new type of partnership for the denomination, there are many details that need to be worked out without bypassing the already established principles. For the missionary, this means, sometimes, lack of clarity as to which are his privileges and responsibilities and which are not. This problem area matures, of course, as the partnership is developed.

2. Sharing Personnel With an Established Mission Agency

Description

The former field director of one of the teams of OC International in Latin America sensed that he wanted to join the work of the international office of COMIBAM. This American missionary agreed to work under the leadership of the president of COMIBAM. This partnership sets a very interesting model, in which the traditional relationship between North American missionaries and Latin American leaders changes. The missionary, traditionally the "boss," comes under the leadership of an Hispanic. This willingness to work under a Latino sets a new pattern of relationship between traditional missions and the newly emerged missions.

Unfortunately, the initial dialogue between OC International and the missionary did not lead to the partnership. The Latin American Mission, however, was able to work out a partnership with COMIBAM International.

Terms of the Partnership

An agreement is established in which this missionary will work under the accountability of COMIBAM, devoting all his ministry to it. The mission will serve as the supporting agency both in matters of finances and in medical and personal care for the missionary.

The financial support of the missionary, both his salary and his ministry expenses, will be raised by the missionary and channeled by Latin American Mission.

Advantages of the Partnership

The experiences of a traditional missionary, with his contacts and relationships, are placed at the service of another missionary movement. This has the value of transferring experience and knowledge to the new generation of missions leaders.

Something remarkable in this partnership is that the leadership of a movement is bonded between the Americanized missionary agency and a Latino-based missionary movement. More than that, this partnership puts to the test the capability of both Latin and American servant-leaders. The Latino leader must work "over" the American missionary, and the American must learn to play a support role, sharing wisdom, experience, gifts, and contacts in his home land, for the purpose of achieving a common goal and establishing the younger missionary movement of Latin America.

Problems

Due to the newness of the partnership, some points of it may be less defined and a bit confusing at times. However, as the partnership develops, some of those issues will be sorted out. The important thing is that there is a mutual willingness from both Latin American Mission and COMIBAM to work things out in order to better serve the partnership.

3. Sharing Common Goals With a Related International Organization

Description

Aware of the need for training new missionaries coming out of Latin America, a partnership has been established between the WEF Missions Commission/International Missionary Training Program and COMIBAM International. Because of shared goals and agenda, both organizations come together to launch a program in the whole continent. The idea is to create awareness of the need for training and to promote the opening of missionary training centers in the different regions and countries of Latin America.

Terms of the Partnership

According to a written document, we agreed to launch a series of consultations in which COMIBAM (in partnership with national COMIBAM groups) will convene and organize, and the WEF Missions Commission will invest the necessary human and material resources to organize such a consultation. Over the course of recent years, the relationship has been developed in such a way that other elements of the COMIBAM agenda have been developed with the help of the WEF Missions Commission and staff.

It is remarkable that during the process of developing this partnership, we have seen the need to change some of the original terms of the agreement and even personnel. The changes have enhanced the richness of the partnership.

Advantages of the Partnership

One of the unique features of this working agreement is that it combines the resources of two international missionary organizations. One is rooted in the Latin American countries; the other has a global outreach. Both offer resources that strengthen each other and therefore further the cause of Christ. The WEF Missions Commission has named a full-time staff member, with long years of experience in Latin America, to a leadership position within COMIBAM International itself. It is not always easy for him to sort out his loyalties, but this creative tension has not proved a disadvantage.

As stated above, this partnership has allowed COMIBAM to expand its vision and potential impact in the continent. This is particularly true not only in the missionary training movement, but also in the production and distribution of strategic missions literature, some of which consists of originally commissioned projects by Latin American authors.

Problems

There are different expectations on both sides. This is especially true regarding the area of accountability. When there is a "big donor" supplying the financial funds, there are expectations and "outcomes" required. These expectations, if not fulfilled, could result in the termination of the partnership. Careful and open discussion of the matter, along with understanding from both sides, is needed to produce beneficial results.

In Conclusion

Partnerships are nice to talk about, but they are not always easy to establish and sustain. Cultural and linguistic issues do not always serve us well. However, in the providence of God, COMIBAM has been able to develop three distinct types of partnerships, each with particular strengths and contributions to make to the Latin American missionary movement. We are thankful to God for all of the specific players who have worked patiently to commit themselves to these partnerships. This is one small but significant evidence of the cooperating international body of Christ.

Rodolfo "Rudy" Girón, from Guatemala, graduated as an architect in 1975. God called him into the ministry in 1979. He is an ordained minister with the Church of God (Cleveland) and has served as an evangelist, pastor, and educator. In 1986, he became involved with COMIBAM (Iberoamerican Congress in Missions) as coordinator for the Caribbean countries. Presently he is the President of COMIBAM and is currently helping to develop the missionary movement among the North American Hispanics.

17

Some Aspects of Partnership in the Summer Institute of Linguistics and Wycliffe Bible Translators

David Cummings

It is impossible to do translation work by oneself, without the help and cooperation of the national speaker of the language. By the very nature of our work in SIL/WBT, we have always been in the partnership mode of operating. We have always acknowledged this, as is evidenced in the credits in our publications.

Terminology

The first essentials in creating a partnership are to *analyze* and then *recognize the distinctives* or uniqueness that each party brings to a given project. Along with the recognition is the need to ensure that each party is using the same meaning for the word. One of the problems in communication is in the area of semantics. When working with our colleagues in Cameroon, they rejected the term "partnership," feeling that it was a very poor concept. After a lot of discussion, we discovered that, with the international banks coercing Cameroon into "partnership" through the investments of the nationals in the country, and then later with the discovery of the high cost of interest for the money loaned in partnership, the nationals strongly resisted our use of the term "partnership."

In the Solomon Islands, we discovered that "consultant" was a very poor choice of word for the people we were sending to help the churches who are doing translation work. The people's only other experience with consultants was that they came and did a study, wrote some articles, left them with some books, and in the meantime spent the greater part of the finances available to the project. Then when the people needed the consultants to "help," no money was available to finish the task. We use the word "advisor" there now, and it is well-accepted. We regard our work as consultative.

"Accountability" can be a very threatening word for both mission boards and national partners. In some instances, it is seen as gross mistrust to talk about such a concept, with many times the failure to realize the legal implications of moving and using money in today's world. A great deal of communication must take place for this term to be seen and understood in its right context.

National Bible Translation Organizations

Over the last 16 years or so, we have been able to encourage or spawn some 16 National Bible Translation Organizations. No two are the same, so variety and flexibility have been a reality for these programs. The following is a brief sampling.

• In Ghana, our whole expatriate team has been led by the local organization, GILLBT, for approximately 15 years. It is their program, and we serve under them.

• In the Solomon Islands, we serve under the Solomon Islands Christian Association. As advisors, we help mother-tongue translators with biblical exegesis, with understanding the biblical culture where applicable, and with such technical aspects as how to handle metaphor, rhetorical questions, etc.

• In India, we are privileged to help the Indian Institute for Cross-Cultural Communication, an arm of the Indian Missions Association. The Institute now has its own academic staff and administration. We continue to frequently send visiting scholars and workshop leaders to assist and advise them in their translation programs.

One of the main lessons we have learned is the length of time it takes to encourage these partnerships. It is not merely the event of signing a partnership contract (if that is applicable), but the total process of constantly working at each phase of the project. This doesn't always sit well with the supporting constituency, who want more speed and more results. This in turn highlights the need for continued education of a constituency which is being fanned along as part of the "info-tainment" culture. Sadly, we are in a world that in its sensationalism is always turning away from the real condition. We in missions have to march to another drumbeat.

Training Nationals to Develop Partnerships

I would like to highlight one other major area in which we are increasingly involved with our national partners. They are beginning to ask us to help them know how to develop their own constituency and relate to the churches and other missions working in their countries. This parallels very much the kind of operation that a home office does for a mission. Our field personnel are well-equipped to teach them the technical side of translation, linguistics, literacy, etc., but by and large they do not feel confident about training them in the skills they need to establish these relationships (partnerships).

We have begun to train the nationals so that they can develop partnerships with their own constituencies, and they have appreciated this help. It would be trite merely to say that since they know their language, their culture, and the whole local scene, they must certainly know how to conduct this aspect of their program in their own country. But in country after country, we have found this not to be the case. And in an endeavor to reduce the training to a principle level, along with the nationals' help, we have named seven functions that they need to address in their home programs:

1. Ministry to the constituency.
2. Public relations.
3. Development of resources.
4. Training.
5. Personnel.
6. Administration.
7. Accountability.

This outline has helped them understand the scope of their responsibility if they are to be effective in relating to their various constituencies.

I believe many new ministries need this kind of help if they are going to be effective for the kingdom in the days ahead. To know one's purpose is one thing, but to have the right structure and *modus operandi* in place can be quite another matter. This happens to be true for the Western mission as well as the non-Western mission.

An Australian, David Cummings worked for six years in the electrical industry before studying theology and beginning his service with Wycliffe in 1957. He served with his wife in Papua New Guinea until returning home to direct the Wycliffe work, first in Australia and later in New Zealand. Elected International President of Wycliffe Bible Translators and Chairman of the Board of Directors in 1981, he has worked with particular interest in partnerships in other countries that lead to establishing National Bible Translation Organizations. He and his wife, Ruth, live in Australia and have four grown children.

18

Mission Kanuri: A Plan of Action for Northern Nigeria

Reuben Ezemadu

The Kanuris, with a population of 3 million or more, are a major ethnic group in northeastern Nigeria. They are a predominant group in Borno and Yobe States of Nigeria (formerly Borno State) and are also to be found in Bauchi and Plateau States, as well as in the neighboring countries of Niger, Chad, and Cameroon.

Islam is predominant among the Kanuris. It has been the state religion for over 800 years. Over 99 percent of the population are Muslims. For the Kanuris, Islam is a way of life. It is central to the family system, culture, learning, and trade. Existing authority and social systems are in full support of Islam. They demonstrate unveiled hostility towards Christianity in particular and towards other religions in general.

Rejection of Islam for a Kanuri may bring about the wrath of family and community. It may result in the death of the convert. Known Kanuri Christians are not more than 20 in number.

A few Christian witness outreaches have been made to Kanuriland, with little impact so far. This survey has, however, shown that mission to Kanuriland is of strategic importance.

In view of the Kanuris' role in the Islamization of Northern Nigeria, their effective conversion may have the potential of a bandwagon effect on the other predominantly Muslim populations in the country.

Mission Objective

General Objective

The Bible declares that the gospel shall be preached in the whole world as a witness to all people groups. The Kanuris will not be an exception. The general objective of Mission Kanuri is to establish a viable Christian witness (a living church) among the Kanuris.

Specific Objectives

1. To share the gospel of our Lord Jesus Christ with 1,500 Kanuris between 1992 and 1995.

2. To disciple 250 Kanuri believers in at least 10 communities by the year 1995.

3. To plant five living churches at the rate of at least one church per year in Kanuriland by 1995.

Strategies

To win Kanuriland for Christ is a task that must be done. We have the force of prophecy to support us. "The kingdoms of this world are become the kingdoms of our Lord, and of His Christ; and He shall reign for ever and ever" (Rev. 11:15).

The following strategies will be employed to achieve our objectives:

1. Prayer

• Mobilization of the church for prayer through our publications, *Mission Focus* and *Prayer Bulletin.*

• Mobilization for prayer in all CMF Chapels, Chapters, and Mission Fields and among all branches of Gospel Bankers and other partners.

2. Integration and Friendship Evangelism

The Kanuris are known to be closed to strangers. They can be won only by long-term friendship and love. Crusades and outdoor preaching may be hazardous. The missionary to the Kanuris must be prepared to learn the ways of the people and be integrated with them.

3. Medical Mission

Health care delivery in northeastern Nigeria is known to be precarious. The demand for better health care can provide a good entry point for mission. A rural health project can be put in place to provide midwifery and dispensary services, among others. More Christian doctors and medical students have expressed interest in missions recently.

4. Multisectoral Team Approach

The missionary team for the Kanuri field should consist of the following:

• A medical couple who should be prepared to serve any-where in the two states.

• A generalist missionary couple.

It would be very helpful if the team could work in close fellowship. In view of the cultural outlook of the Kanuri with respect to unmarried persons, it is strongly recommended that only couples be sent to that field.

Depending on challenges from the field, the missionary team could be strengthened by adding others to the team. There will always be a role for personnel from veterinary, agricultural, and educational missions.

PROGRAM OF WORK				
Activity	**Responsible Person/Agency**	**Requirement**	**Cost**	**Time**
1. PRAYER MOBILIZATION				
CMF Media to publicize Mission Kanuri and to call for prayer	Editor, *Mission Focus, Missions Update, Prayer Bulletin*			Nov-Dec 1991; Jan-Feb 1992
Directive to CMF Chapters, Mission Fields, and Chapels to pray for Mission Kanuri	Director, CMF			Nov-Dec 1991
Directive to Gospel Bankers Branches to pray for Mission Kanuri	President, GB			Nov-Dec 1991
Prayer Conference on Mission Kanuri	Prayer Secretary, CMF			Jan-Feb 1992
2. PLACEMENT OF MISSIONARIES				
Transportation of 2 missionary couples	CMF/GB	Vehicle/fare	N2,000	Apr 1992
Accommodation for missionary team (4 years)	CMF/GB	Rent, household items	N20,000 N10,000	1992-1995
Maintenance for 2 couples for 4 years	CMF/GB	Monthly allowance	N60,000	1992-1995

PROGRAM OF WORK (cont.)				
Activity	Responsible Person/Agency	Requirement	Cost	Time
3. ESTABLISHMENT OF MEDICAL MISSIONS				
Orientation for medical couple at Saki	Dr. Oladoyinbo	Accommo-dation, transport, feeding	N1,500	Mar 1992
Orientation for medical couple at SOM, Idere	Principal, School of Missions	Accommo-dation, transport, feeding	N1,500	Jan 1992
Procurement of equipment, drugs, and materials	Head, Medical Mission	Equipment, drugs, mission transport	N20,000	Apr-Jul 1992
Site for Rural Health Project	Missionary	Rent, upgrading of facilities	N10,000	June 1992

Memorandum of Partnership Understanding

Preamble

The Christian Missionary Foundation Incorporated, hereafter referred to as the CMF, and the Gospel Bankers, Incorporated, hereinafter referred to as GB.

Being desirous of collaborating to fulfill the Great Commission of our Lord Jesus Christ to preach the gospel to all the nations, and coordinating a project of cooperation to establish Christian Mission among the Kanuris of Nigeria, have agreed as follows:

Article 1: Basis of Relationship

1. The Everlasting Scripture, even the Word of God, which reveals the love of God through Jesus Christ, provides the basis for the relationship between CMF and GB. We are the children of God, ambassadors of Christ, and coworkers together with God. We are charged to be perfectly joined together in the same mind and in the same judgment.

2. We are also moved by the Word of God, which reveals the great love of God and His greatest desire to bring all peoples to His saving knowledge. CMF and GB recognize that we can only achieve the goal of world evangelism when we unite our forces, and faith and resources.

Article 2: The Mission Kanuri

Recently surveys have shown clearly that the Kanuri nation of about 3 million are virtually unreached. The Kanuris constitute a pillar of Islam in Nigeria, having been responsible for the introduction and spread of Islam in Northern Nigeria.

The general objective of Mission Kanuri is to establish a viable Christian witness (a living church) among the Kanuris between 1992 and 1995.

Memorandum (cont.)

In spite of past and current attitudes of hostility to Christianity among the Kanuris, the Mission Kanuri is attainable and achievable. Our four-fold strategies are:

   i) Prayer.

   ii) Integration and friendship evangelism.

   iii) Medical mission.

   iv) Multisectoral team approach.

Article 3: Commitment of the CMF

The CMF will bear the following responsibilities:

   i) Recruitment and training of missionary volunteers.

   ii) Commissioning of the missionaries for the mission project. The missionaries shall be given all the entitlements that CMF accords its missionaries.

   iii) Mobilization of prayer for Mission Kanuri.

   iv) Mobilization of financial and other resources for the project.

   v) Supervision and visitation of missionaries on the field.

   vi) Regular monitoring and evaluation of the project through receipt of field reports from missionaries.

Article 4: Commitment of GB

The GB will bear the following responsibilities:

   i) Co-commissioning of the missionaries for the mission project.

   ii) Mobilization of prayer for Mission Kanuri.

   iii) Mobilization of financial resources for the project.

   iv) Provision of funds for the execution of the project.

Memorandum (cont.)

v) Supervision and visitation of missionaries on the field.

vi) Regular monitoring and evaluation of the project through receipt of field reports from missionaries.

Article 5: Management of Mission Kanuri Project

A joint Management Board of both CMF and GB will be set up to manage and oversee the Mission Kanuri Project. Its membership will be drawn from both organizations, which will supply four members each.

The Director of CMF shall be Chairman of the Board, while the President of GB shall be Vice-Chairman. The Secretary of the Board shall be the Field Secretary of CMF, while the Treasurer shall be drawn from GB.

Reuben E. Ezemadu is the current Chairman of the Nigeria Evangelical Missions Association (NEMA) and the secretary of the Third World Missions Association (TWMA). He is also the Director of The Christian Missionary Foundation (CMF) in Nigeria and a member of the WEF Missions Commission. He is married and has four children.

19

Towards Interdependent Partnership: WEC in Multiple Partnerships

Dietrich Kuhl

Worldwide Evangelization for Christ (WEC) is an international, interdenominational faith mission, founded in 1913 by Charles Thomas Studd, one of England's outstanding cricketers. He joined Hudson Taylor's China Inland Mission (CIM; today OMF) and worked for 10 years in China (1885-1895). WEC International has been modeled to quite a degree after the principles of the CIM. Today WEC has about 1,500 workers from 41 different nationalities, serving in 57 countries on all six continents. About 140 of the missionaries are from Two Thirds World countries. Emphasis is on targeting the remaining unreached peoples.

WEC International is cooperating with about 250 partners worldwide (churches, missions, and associations). The degree of formality varies. Not all partnerships are on the basis of a formal cooperation agreement. We are committed to partnership, to putting the kingdom first, and to Dr. George W. Peters' advice at the 1971 Green Lake Consultation, to avoid being a "churchless mission."

Since the mid-1950s, WEC leadership has pursued models of passing on the missionary vision to Asian, African, and Latin

American Christians and churches. The aim was to mobilize this great potential for world mission. It was felt that it was not enough to involve WEC-related churches in local or regional evangelism, which had been done from the beginning. The completion of the missionary task can only be achieved if all join hands. The aim was to establish so-called "Centers for Fellowship and Outreach," WEC's CFO Program. These centers could be indigenous missions, mission departments of WEC-related churches, or WEC sending bases in non-Western countries. WEC wanted to be flexible and not force a rigid concept on others. Various models have evolved.

Mission/Mission Partnership

1. WEC and Indonesian Missionary Fellowship (IMF) in Batu, East Java: Cooperation in Indonesia (since IMF's founding in 1959), Brazil, Germany, and The Gambia. An official Cooperation Agreement was signed much later (October 1980).

2. WEC and Calvary Ministries, Nigeria: Cooperation in The Gambia, church planting among the Susu in Guinea (joint venture), CAPRO's School of Mission in Abidjan, printing presses in UK and Nigeria, research, and possibly cooperation in Benin.

3. WEC and Margaya Missionary Society in Sri Lanka.

4. Local and national multi-agency cooperation (strategic alliances) in an increasing number of countries.

5. Assistance in the formation of Antioch Mission in Brazil, an indigenous mission under Brazilian leadership from the beginning.

6. Assistance in the formation of the Korean West African Mission (e.g., apprenticeship training of its leader for two years in The Gambia).

7. A variety of bilateral mission/mission secondment agreements.

8. An agreement with International Nepal Fellowship (INF) to represent it in some of WEC's sending base countries and to process workers.

Conclusions

1. Partnership relations with other missions generally worked very well. Often we could achieve more in partnership than each one of us could have achieved alone.

2. Partnership is not static. It goes through stages. This has to do with changing personalities, group dynamics, and changing situational factors.

3. Leaders of multicultural teams need special orientation.

4. Good and open communication, trust, and patience are essential.

5. Partnership and cooperation in Restricted Access Nations (RANs) or Creative Access Nations (CANs) is a must. We need facilitators for such strategic alliances. Missions should recruit "missionary diplomats" for such leadership tasks in multicultural and multi-agency partnerships. They need special gifts and training.

Mission/Church Partnership

1. Cooperation Agreements with various Korean churches:

• The General Assembly of Presbyterian Church in Korea (GAPCK, Haptong): Secondment of a Korean worker for two years (see point 6 under "Mission/Mission Partnership" above).

• The Korean Presbyterian Church (Reformed) (KPCR, Ge Hyuk Reformed Church): Secondment of workers for Indonesia (did not work out for reasons beyond the Church's and WEC's control).

• General Assembly of Presbyterian Church in Korea (Kosin Reformed Church): Secondment of workers for Ghana.

2. Cooperation Agreement between WEC and Pasir Panjang Hill Brethren Chapel (PPHBC), Singapore: Assistance in their modular missionary training program and possible channeling of workers.

3. Cooperation Agreement between WEC and the Sino-Mauritian Church in Mauritius: Five of their workers joined WEC International for ministry in Fiji, Côte d'Ivoire, Senegal, and Greece.

4. More and more local congregations want to be more involved in sending out their missionaries. Missions need to be more flexible in the areas of candidate selection, placement, and decision making with regard to meaningful involvement of churches.

Assistance in Establishing a Mission Department in WEC-Related Churches

1. CECCA 16 Church in Zaire sent their first missionaries to Côte d'Ivoire in 1987. It is a very successful church/church/mission cooperation. Another couple will join the work in Chad.

2. Evangelical Crusade Church in Colombia sent a missionary couple to Uruguay in 1978 to continue the WEC work there, now aided by Brazilian WEC workers.

Cooperation With Associations

1. WEC and Korean Partnership Mission Fellowship (KPMF): This agreement will be transferred to the newly founded Korean World Mission Association (KWMA).

2. Inter-mission agreement with Association of Evangelicals in Africa and Madagascar (AEAM), with the aim of producing TV/video programs for francophone Africa.

3. Cooperation Agreement with Ghana Evangelism Committee (GEC) and secondment of workers (DAWN project).

Establishment of Indigenous WEC Sending Bases in Non-Western Countries

1. Brazil (Missao AMEM): About 45 Brazilian workers.

2. Singapore: 15 workers and another 16 in the pipeline.

3. Hong Kong: 12 workers.

These three indigenous WEC sending bases are self-governing and cooperate with WEC worldwide in a federative system on the basis of the same basic principles, though not necessarily according to the same forms and practices. There are growing pains, but we are convinced that the system works well and is a blessing to both sides.

Conclusions

1. Multicultural teams have their own dynamics. At times, cultural aspects or misunderstandings can aggravate personality issues. At times, personality issues are mistaken for cultural issues. WEC has established a Multicultural Working Group to prepare orientation material for our multicultural teams.

2. Good prefield preparation and field orientation are essential; so is leadership training.

3. Missionary candidates need to be assessed to see whether they will be able to function in a multicultural team. Teachability is the key. Not everyone will be able to cope with multicultural teamwork. We need to be realistic.

Partnership in Training Non-Western Missionaries (by Multicultural Staff)

1. About one-third of the 90 students at WEC's three-year Missionary Training College in Australia come from Asian countries.

2. An increasing number of students at WEC's new three-year Missionary Training College in Holland (English-medium instruction) are from non-Western countries.

3. A high proportion of students at WEC's modular Missionary Orientation Centre in England were from non-Western countries (now transferred to All Nations Christian College, UK).

4. WEC missionaries have given assistance in the training of missionaries in Japan (Ken Roundhill) and Korea (Dr. Patrick McElligott).

5. Indonesian Bible Institute of the Indonesian Missionary Fellowship in Batu/East Java. WEC has been involved in the training of Indonesian missionaries and evangelists since the establishment of the Indonesian Bible Institute in 1959.

6. WEC's Latin American Missionary Training College in Montes Claros, Brazil, has a multicultural staff under Brazilian leadership and an increasingly multicultural student body.

Conclusion

A multicultural student body and teaching staff seem to be ideal for cross-cultural missionary training.

Conclusions

1. I believe that cooperation, wherever possible, is pleasing to our Lord as we move together in ways which bring glory to Jesus Christ, the Lord of the harvest. This picture of the harvest implies close cooperation and joining of hands. It is His harvest, not the churches' or missions'. The loving unity of a multicultural team is a powerful testimony to the love and power of the Lord of the harvest.

2. The most important ingredients for cooperation seem to be flexibility, teachability, humility, patience, and mutual trust. In short, it is the message of the cross and the power of the Holy Spirit which bind us together.

3. Although I understand and share the concern for equality, I prefer the biblical emphasis on humility over the secular idea of equality (Phil. 2:1-8). Equality seems to be concerned with self and our rights. Humility is based on servanthood and living for the glory of God.

A medical doctor born in Germany, Dietrich Kuhl served as a missionary in Indonesia from 1972 to 1986 with WEC and the Indonesian Missionary Fellowship. For 11 years, he was involved full-time in teaching and training Indonesian pastors and missionaries. In 1987, he became International Director of WEC International, located in England. Married to a medical doctor, he has two daughters at university.

20

An Indian Missions
Partnership Model

Ebe Sunder Raj

About 10 years ago, some of the Indian leaders in our mission fields felt the need for a unique partnership. They recognized that there was a gap between the field evangelists/missionaries and the Christian mass media in India. The Christian media built gospel awareness and interest in the hearts of millions of non-Christians. There are about 1 million inquiries per year from interested persons. But there was no way to link the interested persons with the evangelists/pastors on the ground. The media centers were not aware which evangelist was working where.

The IMA Annual Conference in 1984 focused on this need of follow-up. This resulted in the 1985 Consultation at Yavatmal, where leaders from 23 organizations (media and missions) met and evolved a network model. This model was tried out in Orissa for two years (1990-1991) under the Orissa State Committee. This Committee consists of state level leaders of all the major missions and churches in Orissa. The Committee, along with IMA's Assistant Coordinator, directed this network of 45 mission groups and denominations in Orissa state.

Training Camps on Follow-Up

The Committee first identified the location of 1,200 evangelists, pastors, and missionaries in Orissa state. Half of them underwent a two-day training camp on follow-up. These training camps were conducted in every district headquarters of Orissa in 1990. The training was given by the state leaders of missions in Orissa.

All the media centers who have a media program in Orissa started sending their seekers' addresses. The total came to 14,000 addresses. Of these addresses, many were old, incomplete, or inaccurate, but 6,000 of these were sorted out by the computer and sent to the nearest evangelist, pastor, or missionary for personal follow-up. Of them 80 percent were non-Christian seekers. Amar Jyoti of India took the responsibility to enroll all of the seekers in a Bible study course by correspondence.

Seekers Camps

After about three months of personal follow-up, seekers camps were conducted in each district of Orissa. These seekers camps were conducted and financed by the joint effort of the missions and churches in Orissa, along with IMA. A very keen and committed veterinary surgeon met the major part of this expense.

The evangelists and pastors from the respective districts were present in the district level seekers camp to take care of the follow-up of the seekers who made decisions at the camp.

The feedback from these seekers as to their spiritual growth was sent to the respective media agency.

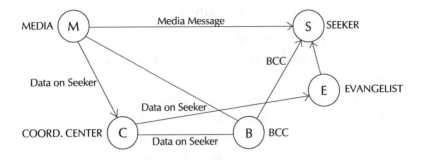

Now, after the completion of one round of camps, the responsibility of continuing this work is turned over to the local leadership. The role of IMA in this was only to build a model which can be carried on by local state leadership and also be emulated by other states.

IMA has now the necessary software which can be used by any state network and by any major national level media agency for follow-up.

Limitations

What were the limitations?

1. Even though the cooperation and partnership were very encouraging, the achievement could have been much higher if all the agencies with a potential role had cooperated in this partnership. Others were very slow to respond.

2. Some media groups do not seem to take follow-up as a serious business. Most seem to be content solely with broadcasting or distribution of literature. Some media centers did not maintain a current list of their own recent seekers. This hindered follow-up.

Blessings

What were the blessings?

1. For the first time in India, an effective network model for follow-up was built.

2. More than the immediate statistical results achieved, which were very, very small, the greatest blessing was working together with so many organizations and churches.

This partnership was not limited merely to follow-up. The State Committee often found itself discussing persecution, comity, and other common issues affecting the churches and missions in Orissa.

An Indian citizen, Ebenezer Sunder Raj has two degrees in engineering. He served first with Operation Mobilization in India and then for 11 years as All India Field Director of the Friends Missionary Prayer Band. In 1986, he became General Secretary of India Missions Association, the national federation for 54 Indian missions and over 3,500 missionaries working in all the states of India and eight other countries. He is an author of missions books and a member of the WEF Missions Commission.

21

OC International in an Indian Partnership

Larry Keyes

Worldwide, one person in seven is an Indian. The population (820 million) is growing so fast that it is estimated India will be over 1 billion people by 1994! This large population represents both an urgent challenge and a great opportunity for world evangelization.

Within India's 23 states, there are at least 600,000 villages which need to be reached with the gospel. The Christian message continues to make gains in India's south and northeast (the State of Kerala in the south is 22 percent Christian, and the State of Meghalaya in the northeast is estimated at 65 percent Christian). But very little progress is being made in the vast regions and very populous parts of India's north. The State of Uttar Pradesh in the north, for example, has so many people (138 million) that only seven nations in the world have a greater population, but it is only 0.15 percent Christian. Or, the northern State of Bihar has a greater population than Great Britain (65 million), but it is only 1.17 percent Christian.

Although all of India continues to need an effective evangelistic witness, our own research within the country during 1982-1983 indicated the greatest and most urgent need to be in India's 10 northern states. It is here where the leadership of OC International (OC) started to focus interest and prayer.

A Brief History of the Developing Partnership

For several decades, the Christian leadership within India has given opportunities for ministry to various missionaries with OC International. Sports Ambassadors, OC's evangelistic sports ministry, sent several basketball and soccer teams to present the gospel message in many cities. Members of OC's International Ministry Team (IMT) have conducted a number of pastors conferences, and other OC leaders have participated in many national missionary and church growth conventions.

During this time of short visits and quick-impact ministries, we acknowledged it was impossible for foreigners (non-Indian missionaries) to obtain permanent visas or long-term work permits due to governmental restrictions. We also realized it was very difficult for the Christians living in the unreached areas of India's north to evangelize the whole, vast region themselves—or to do so even with the help of many faithful mission groups from India's southern region. It was our impression that a great number of Christian workers serving in India's north needed both encouragement and additional assistance in order for the 315 million people in the northern states to hear and effectively receive the gospel message. For this assistance to materialize, hundreds of additional missionaries had to be recruited either from India's southern states or from India's Christian northeast (or both).

With this challenge, various leaders within OC started to pray. We neither knew how or with whom we could work. But the challenge to help the Christians within India to reach north India remained firm. God began to answer our prayer in two phases: the first focused upon a cooperative agreement with an Indian denomination in order to partner with a very capable missionary statesman from Northeast India; the second focused upon a partnership with a training center as one result of the missionary's ministry.

Phase One: Partnership With the Nagaland Baptist Church

In 1984, I met Rev. Phuveyi Dozo. At the time, he was General Secretary of the Nagaland Missionary Movement of the Nagaland Baptist Church. He had been responsible for the recruitment and training of hundreds of missionaries who were deployed from Nagaland (Northeast India) to various surrounding nations (China, Burma, Bangladesh) and to various northern states within India. He was completing a doctorate in northern California and, during several months, we were able to meet together and discuss the challenges of India. It became apparent that God had brought us together.

Through two years' time, Dr. Phuveyi Dozo and OC developed a strong mutual trust and common vision. He and his wife attended OC conferences in the Philippines and Singapore, and later in our international headquarters in the States.

In November 1986 and January 1987, two trips were planned to visit Nagaland and establish a more formal relationship with the General Council of the Nagaland Baptist Church (NBC). Both Dr. Dozo and I wanted to work together in evangelizing North India. In order to do so, we thought a formal relationship between the NBC and OC would significantly strengthen the effort. This partnership venture was primarily focused upon Dr. Dozo and his family.

The partnership would enable the sending of the Dozo family from Kohima to Delhi—a true cross-cultural endeavor. Both NBC and OC would be involved in their financial support and ministry encouragement. The partnership would also develop a channel where other Naga missionaries could be sent from Nagaland to North India and where Dr. Dozo would provide orientation to those missionaries. In order to develop this new type of cooperative venture (new to both NBC and OC), both Dr. Dozo and I tried to obtain the necessary permission from India's federal government for my travel to Kohima, Nagaland. Meetings were planned for those days, and formal agreements were expected to be discussed. However, since the mid-1950s, that region has been restricted to foreigners. Permission was not granted on either occasion, and the meetings were not held.

In light of this difficulty, a letter was sent to the Nagaland Baptist Church Council on February 17, 1987, outlining two suggested options for the formal partnership. Because of that letter and other correspondence, the Nagaland Baptist Church Council Executive Committee recommended on August 20, 1987, that Dr. Dozo's family be fully released from NBC responsibilities in order to partner with OC in missions—a recommendation that was formally approved at the annual General Council in January 1988 (on the occasion of the church's 50th anniversary).

To further clarify the partnership with the NBC Council, Dr. Charles Holsinger and I (from OC) met with Dr. Dozo and Rev. Alem-meren (from the NBC Council) in Calcutta on January 27, 1988. We agreed that the partnership would consist of the following basic points:

Responsibilities for the NBCC

1. Prayer support for OC and our other ministries in India. (They will list several of our prayer requests in their monthly bulletins.)

2. Promotion of the OC team in India through NBCC channels.

3. Recruitment of missionaries to plant churches in the unreached areas within India that are suggested by OC.

4. Financial support of Phuveyi Dozo and his family.

Responsibilities for OC

1. Provide leadership training among NBCC missionaries.

2. Allow Dr. Dozo to minister in Northeast India, pending need and availability.

3. Send OC literature to NBCC personnel, helping them to understand church growth, missions, and evangelism.

4. Provide information to NBCC on areas of need and strategies that are to be used (or that are being used) within India.

Phase Two: Partnership With the Outreach Leadership Training Center

The following declaration by the Nagaland Baptist Church initiated their strong missionary effort.

Today, the 15th of October, 1977, Nagaland Baptist Church Council had taken one of the most historic actions in the history of Nagaland Churches. Today NBCC had inaugurated the Mission of World Evangelization. From today, the task of world evangelization is started. NBCC is enlisting 10,000 volunteers for this noble cause. You can enlist your name or your family for this cause. You can enlist your name to fulfill the task of world evangelization by:

1. Going out to the unreached regions....

2. Witnessing to the saving power of Christ where you are.

3. Praying for the lost souls and studying God's Word....

4. Supporting the Movement with willing contributions....

The partnership with OC in releasing Dr. Phuveyi and Ave Dozo and family for broader ministry within India is part of the application of this declaration. The support of the newly established Outreach Leadership Training Center (OLTC) in Dimapur, Nagaland, is also part of the results of this declaration.

On March 30, 1992, Rev. Greg Gripentrog (OC Director for Asia) and I were finally allowed by India's national government to travel into the restricted region of Northeast India. We were able to meet many of the people with whom we had established a partnership. On March 31, 1992, we laid the foundation stone for the Outreach Leadership Training Center, and on April 1, 1992, we participated in its inauguration.

The purpose of the OLTC is to train 1,000 missionaries by A.D. 2000, who will plant churches in North India. Besides the encouragement received from the NBCC and related churches, the OLTC received support from the Assembly of God, Nagaland Revival Church, Nagaland Baptist Revival Churches, the Dimapur Pentecostal Church, and OC International. Our partnership with OLTC came initially through Dr. Dozo and later became more formal through our visit last March 30 through April 3.

In the words of Rev. Dr. V. Epao, Director of the OLTC:

> The OLTC has made a target for outreach. India has a population of nearly a billion, out of which hardly 3 percent is Christian—most [of the Christians are in] Kerala, Nagaland, and Mizoram. Of the unreached regions, North India [and] especially Uttar Pradesh is the least reached, having a population of 138 million with only 0.15 percent Christian.... Adjoining states such as Bihar, Madhya Pradesh, Haryana, Punjab, and Himachal Pradesh are unreached.

This goal is in line with OC's interests and early prayers. By contributing toward the success of this missionary training center, we are able to help evangelize North India through national workers.

Our involvement with OLTC is in four areas:

1. Dr. Dozo and other OC personnel will help in the educational training of the 1,000 missionaries at the training center in Dimapur.

2. Those missionaries who are sent to North India will receive an additional short period of contextualized training at Khatima, Uttar Pradesh. This will be coordinated by Dyaram Singh, a Naga missionary.

3. Dr. Dozo will continue to suggest locations for future church planting activities to OLTC missionaries and NBCC workers.

4. Dr. Dozo and other OC personnel will continue to be consultants or advisors to OLTC and NBCC missionaries

concerning the best and most effective strategies to reach North India for Christ.

The next eight years will be exciting as we work in partnership with those involved in the OLTC and with the missionaries coming from the Naga churches. Our partnership will be reviewed each year so that measures could be taken to strengthen this relationship. Our desire is to continue working with our colleagues in India for many years. We trust that hundreds of new churches will be planted through this effort, and we hope that more qualified Indian missionaries will join our team in Delhi. We pray that North India will be further reached with the gospel of Christ by being a part of Dr. Dozo's ministry and that of the OLTC.

Dr. Larry E. Keyes joined OC International (OC) in 1971. He ministered in Brazil for 11 years, focusing upon Two Thirds World missions and publishing a book on the subject. He is President of the Evangelical Fellowship of Mission Agencies (EFMA) and has been President of OC International for 10 years. Dr. Keyes and his wife, Shirley, make their home in Colorado Springs, Colorado. They have two children, both in college and preparing for missionary involvement.

Conclusions

22

Partners Into the Next Millennium

William D. Taylor

What more needs to be said? We have seen the biblical foundation for partnership. We have analyzed the essence of partnership. We have argued the hot issues in partnership. We have evaluated many partnership models. So what more must be done?

Next Steps

First, we must see partnerships as God sees them. He is the author of cooperation, modeling it within the Trinity and by delegating the major mandates to His people, partners with us in history, both with Israel and the church. Partnerships are rooted in the nature of God and therefore are crucial elements in our life and ministry, revealing our interdependence and unity in Christ—a key witness to the world.

Second, we must see the great benefits of partnerships. This means dealing frankly with apprehensions some may have. For too many years, I worked under individualistic and separatist leadership whose attitude to partnerships seemed to be, "We don't need them and they don't need us!" But let's be realistic. We fear the loss of what we consider biblical priorities, the loss of power and control, the loss of our own focused personnel projects, the loss of key team members to other organizations, the loss of cultural distinctives. Then the benefits emerge as we seriously understand synergy directed by the Holy Spirit.

Third, there are frustrated and failed partnerships. We must be realistic about these, face the truth, and analyze the history of failed cooperative ministry projects. Too many times we have emphasized the glorious benefits of working together and have not dealt with the realities. Some might say, "Then why enter into more partnerships?" Simply because of the hundreds of positive models currently operating on the various fields of the world, which can be evaluated and learned from. For every bad case, I now know of five good ones. And all partnerships, even the best ones, struggle with a cluster of problems: personal pride and agenda, personality conflicts, cultural variants, inadequate personal relationships upon which to build trust, differing expectations and guidelines for measuring results. We have attempted to deal forthrightly in this book with at least some of these issues.

Fourth, our church and mission leadership must take deliberate steps to commit to and enter into careful partnerships. The possibilities are almost limitless, if we have the dedication to change the way we have done things. We do not "push partnerships" for their sake only. We urge the development of these creative relationships, because our world's need calls for them, and because Jesus is glorified by them, and because the world sees tangible demonstrations of unity in the body of Christ. Partnerships are a means of proclaiming the centrality and singularity of our Lord in ways that draw people to Jesus.

The Significant Partnership Players

All of us who are committed to and involved in cross-cultural ministry must evaluate specific areas of potential partnerships, discover if there are already parallel relationships that are instructive, and then move into action. Let me mention three specific categories for partnership.

First of all, in every continent and in most countries, local churches in mission have a wealth of opportunities. Every church is a training/sending base for global evangelism. Unfortunately, too many churches desire to go it alone in missions, even attempting to place long-term staff in restricted access nations. Part of the problem is a faulty understanding of the church at Antioch, seeing it simply as a classic sending church. Another difficulty is that these churches try to send their teams without serious commitment to three major dimensions: comprehensive prefield training (including biblical and theological study); long-term language and culture learning; and on-field shepherding, strategizing, and supervising. The best church partnerships that I know of accept the contribution that formal Bible/theology/missions schools can offer their missionaries, and they are actively partnering with another church or have entered into partnership with an on-field mission agency with experience in that ministry. In some cases, the church team has been seconded to the agency. In other cases, the partnership develops with a national church.

Secondly, agencies have singular opportunities to share resources for the advance of the kingdom of God and His Christ. There is no need to expand this theme, due to the fact that so much of this book applies clearly to mission agencies in partnership.

Thirdly, national and regional mission associations have a wide-open partnership door, as illustrated in some of the models here presented. These relationships are between the association and agencies, between Western and non-Western associations, between churches and associations. The World Evangelical Fellowship Missions Commission not only promotes these covenants, but tries to model them with its own active partnerships.

Many other players and combinations will emerge. May we have the grace to act on what we already know.

Peering Beyond the Year 2000
Into the Next Millennium

Reading the most recent edition of Patrick Johnstone's monumental *Operation World* leaves me thrilled, yearning, and sobered at the same time. I am thrilled to read and sense the phenomenal advance of the gospel, even since the earlier edition of this invaluable book. God has truly done great things, and we rejoice at the growth in number and quality of those who will join to worship the Lamb. I am left yearning for the coming of Christ, the Savior who has waited so patiently for His church to obey both the Great Commission and the Great Commandment. The depth and breadth of misery, corruption, oppression, and evil supernaturalism at work in the world stagger me. I am sobered when I realize the immensity of the task remaining. I would drop in despair, were it not for my understanding of the magnificent sovereignty of God and His purposes for His earth.

Only God knows what is in store for the world and for the church committed to world evangelization. Within short years, if Christ tarries His glorious return, we will slip with varied degrees of fanfare into the next millennium. The church of Christ already has the resources for total world evangelism. But if we go our individualistic ways, we will only fragment our resources, our spirit, and the desires of the Spirit of God.

The recent experience of the former Soviet Empire is worthy of a brief comment. It is hard to imagine that for a mere handful of years those doors were sealed against open proclamation of Christ. Some of those doors are turning out to be revolving ones, and today's easy access is tomorrow's restricted access. But when the opportunity arose, those nations were flooded by over 1,000 Western Christian movements invading that area with their particular message and distinctives. Many competing groups hired the same translators, who at times had to communicate a biblical message one month and a heretical message the next month. Too many Western groups blitzed Russia with high-cost programs, with limited or non-existent regard for Russian culture or the existing churches already there, and with no concern for learning the heart-language of the people. We are learning some hard lessons from this experience, and while we glory in the advance of the gospel, not always was this done properly or with good motives.

Now what about mainland China? If and when the "old ruling men" die off, and assuming there is new liberty to proclaim the gospel—even by non-Chinese—what will the rest of the Christian world do? Will we invade China like the former USSR? Will we disregard the Chinese Christian leadership in the mainland, which has paid the highest cost for following Christ? How will we listen to Chinese leadership in places like Hong Kong or Taiwan? Will we cooperate under and with mission agencies with a long trajectory of ministry to the Chinese people? In other words, can we do it differently this time?

The powerful surges of the Holy Spirit in Africa, Asia, Latin America, the South Pacific, the Caribbean, and the Middle East must be considered. Countries once considered mission fields that received missionaries are now mission sending bases. The privilege and task of global evangelization are truly interna-tionalized, even though the power structures are not yet. European and North American churches cannot blithely go on our merry way without considering the agenda concerns of our mature colleagues in the so-called non-Western world. One clear partnership implication for me is that cross-cultural servants and churches from the North Atlantic nations must demonstrate a learning spirit to work under Africans, Asians, and Latins. We in the West do not have the right to call the shots, set the agenda, or control the program by our finances. Partnership will have a great variety of color and culture shades!

Ponder the restricted access nations, a reality true for most of the countries in the 10/40 Window. The strategic placement of gifted, called, equipped, and proactively sent tentmakers is an imperative. But who has experience in this? Thank God, there are ministries with a vast history and involvement exactly in these specialized ministries. And not only from the West. Some of the most creative tentmaking done today in these sensitive nations is being done by Koreans. Can we cooperate with them, or at least listen to the way God has led them? And will the Koreans listen to and learn from the rest of the body of Christ with experience in this area?

A Final Word

"Just do it!" That public relations slogan reverberates in certain societies advertising a certain kind of sports shoe. But in some ways, that is how I feel about partnerships. Just do them! Obviously, not without consensus, not without prayer, not without careful preparation, not without counting the cost. In God's providence, there are organizations with experience in brokering and guiding partnerships.

May God give us the grace to move ahead as we should. Just do it!

Appendices

Appendices

APPENDIX 1
Definition of Terms

Two are better than one because they have a good return for their labor. For if either of them falls, the one will lift up his companion. But woe to the one who falls when there is not another to lift him up. Furthermore, if two lie down together they keep warm, but how can one be warmed? And if one can overpower him who is alone, two can resist him. A cord of three strands is not quickly torn apart.

— Ecclesiastes 4:9-12

1. ***Cooperation/Teamwork.*** Working together for a common purpose. There are different degrees or levels of cooperation. Some projects require a great degree of cooperation and others not much at all. Three characteristics describe cooperation and its greatest impact. "First, they must be relevant. The end results must be closely tied to the ultimate purposes of each individual or organization in the group. Secondly, the benefits must be of sufficient magnitude to make it worth the effort. Finally, the individual team members must really believe these benefits are achievable" (P. MacMillan).

2. ***Networking/Networks.*** Networking takes place when similar individuals or groups pool resources for the greater

243

advancement of the common objective, sharing information, ideas, and resources.

"Networks are people talking to each other, sharing ideas, information, and resources" (J. Naisbitt). Networking is a verb, not a noun, and basically is a means of connecting people with one another. "Networks can go beyond the mere transfer of data and become a means of actually creating and exchanging knowledge. Networking is invariably on an informal basis, but it becomes more efficient and fruitful when people acknowledge its presence, engender its activity, and actively respond to the overtures of others in the network. What can we share?... We can talk about good ideas, new strategies and structures of evangelism, of teaching, training, or whatever other concept we, as individual foundations, discover and support" (P. MacMillan).

3. ***Partnership.*** Using mutual gifts to accomplish tasks.

4. ***Joint Ventures/Strategic Alliances.*** "Here is where two or more organizations join together in a more formal relationship to accomplish a specific goal or purpose. Joint ventures incorporate a higher degree of commitment than networking and the exchange of information. Here, greater levels of resources are invested. They're not always financial in nature; it might be that one organization... has expertise or manpower needed by the other. The other might resource the project with finances, while the second or the third does so with expertise or manpower. Regardless, the level of investment is higher and the relationship more formal" (P. MacMillan).

5. ***Synergism.*** "Synergism occurs when the output is greater than the sum of the inputs. For example, using an illustration from nature, one draft horse can pull four tons. If you harnessed two draft horses together, they can pull 22 tons. That is synergism!" (P. MacMillan).

6. ***Guidelines for Effective Partnerships.*** R. Kanter writes that successful cooperative relationships are characterized by the following three elements: the relationship is

important; the partners are interdependent; and each partner is fully informed.

7. **Categories of Partnership.** Tokunboh Adeyemo presents eight current partnership models, casting his vote for the eighth one.

7-1. *Mother/Daughter Model.* Mission agencies plant churches and maintain an ongoing relationship with the national church. As it were, the mission agency "drives the car" until the national church is old enough to "take the wheel"; the two then "switch seats." Definite tensions can arise in this arrangement. Frequently the Western agency wants to manipulate, and the national church resists domination. The two are brothers, but the agency is an "older" brother whom the national church must consult. The "umbilical cord" is not completely cut.

7-2. *Parachurch Establishment (Entrepreneurial) Model.* Under this model, parachurch relief and/or evangelism agencies set up their own structure and hire nationals to carry out the objectives of the enterprise. Among nationals there is a growing unrest and frustration with this system; some radical young evangelicals call this process "renting the nationals." They feel like decorations on the cake, added for show so that agencies can boast of their national force.

7-3. *National Support Model.* Here, Western agencies and churches arrange direct financial support for nationals and their projects. Initially this model seemed to be the catch-all solution. Then we discovered that partnership is more than just giving money. Some nationals feel used to fulfill somebody else's agenda.

7-4. *Nationals-on-the-Team Model.* This model incorporates nationals working side by side with Westerners, and nationals must raise their own support to be part of the team. Many churches in the West still are very reluctant to accept the national as part of themselves.

7-5. *Paternal Network Model.* Here, the indigenous mission agency requests assistance from its international counterpart.

7-6. *Secondment Model.* Under this model, a Western church or mission agency seconds, or loans, its personnel to a national church for a period of time. A variant of this is when the Western body financially supports national personnel under a three- to five-year program, with a yearly scaling down of Western funds as the national organization or church picked up the responsibility.

7-7. *Empowerment Model.* Western agencies supply the money, personnel, and technical assistance needed by national churches. Rather than setting up its own structure, the agency empowers national churches to do the work. This model is being used more by relief and development ministries.

7-8. *Multinational Church Network (Enablement) Model.* Under this model, partners enable each other as members of the same body. The supporting Western church does not act merely as camouflage for the Third World church's work; ownership does not lie in either party's hand. This model presupposes that neither the Western nor the Third World church has all it needs to fulfill the scriptural mandate; there is an acknowledgement of mutual need. Here mission and vision are church-rooted. We thank God for parachurch organizations, but it is not His desire to replace the church with parachurch structures. Here partnership and control of property belong to nationals. Partnership springs from love, which allows them to disagree. For nationals do not exist merely to rubber stamp Western ideas and decisions. Here there is true knowledge and discernment of the people and their real needs. Partnership is more than money. It means the sharing of God-given resources—money, people, experience, and knowledge. Here there are integrity and honesty.

8. **Roadblocks to Effective Partnership.** P. MacMillan suggests seven of the most common barriers.

8-1. *Benefits.* "If the benefits of cooperation are unclear or perceived to be insufficient or unachievable, then our cooperative effort will invariably be plagued by anemia of the spirit."

8-2. *Agenda.* The "agenda barrier" looks at central purpose. "If the alignment between the individual purpose and that highlighted by the cooperative effort is not clear or complete, individual team members will begin pulling in different directions. Teaming up is not automatic, and it depends to a large extent on our ability to align personal and organizational goals and purposes.

8-3. *Lack of Trust.* This lack among partners, "...either in motive or competency, makes us hesitant to become interdependent."

8-4. *Strategy.* This barrier may arise if certain efforts or plans do not require teamwork.

8-5. *Lack of Skills.* We might want to partner but do not have the specific abilities to do it properly. This brings confusion instead of success.

8-6. *Uneven Level of Commitment.* At times there may be an uneven level of commitment between the partners. For one party, the partnership may be central; for the other, it may be secondary—a prescription for chaos.

8-7. *Imbalance of Benefits.* This barrier arises when it appears that one partner stands to gain more than the other.

APPENDIX 2

Agreement for Cooperative Work Between a New Partner Ministry and Partners International (PI)

We believe God has led Partners International of San Jose, California, USA, and (name of new partner ministry) to work cooperatively for the advancement of the gospel. The following guidelines define this partnership.

1. PI will seek funding for the following elements of the New Partner program, including any projects subsequently agreed upon by PI and the New Partner.

2. The purpose and overall goals of these elements of the ministry are: (list)

3. The (operational) plans for the next years in order to reach these goals are: (list)

4. The expected outcomes to be achieved as a result of the carrying out of these plans are: (list)

5. All projects will be documented through the Project Request form or through authorized correspondence.

6. Funds received through PI for the elements above will be transferred to the board of the New Partner through a mutually agreed-upon method.

7. The New Partner will provide PI with a copy of its annual budget no later than one month after the onset of the fiscal year. Each budget should include anticipated expenses and income with PI listed as a subcategory.

8. The New Partner may appeal for assistance from various sources in the USA or in other countries. However, in those countries where PI has an associated council (Australia, Canada, Japan, New Zealand, the United Kingdom, and the United States of America), appeals will be carefully coordinated with PI. For appeals made in countries where there is no associated council, the New Partner will send copies of correspondence to PI.

9. The New Partner will provide the reports and information necessary for PI fundraising, representation, and services. Selected workers will participate in the Sponsor-A-National Program as a means of raising monthly support for the New Partner.

10. PI will maintain a mailing list on behalf of the New Partner for all contacts outside of the USA.

11. A worker of the New Partner wishing to include in his/her prayer letter an appeal for contributions towards a project will first obtain approval from the New Partner board and the International Operations Office.

12. PI's Regional Coordinator is recognized as the authorized representative of PI in all relations with the partner ministry, and the partner ministry will cooperate with the Regional Coordinator in all matters pertaining to this working agreement.

13. The New Partner will make available to PI necessary financial records at the site of the partner ministry for internal auditing purposes no more frequently than once every two (2) years. PI will provide written audited procedures to the New Partner at least ninety (90) days in advance of the auditor's visit.

14. The undersigned agree with the PI Statement of Faith without reservation.

15. The partnership between PI and the New Partner will be guided by the attached document titled "Principles and Policies for Cooperative Work."

16. This agreement will expire no later than (stated date), or at an earlier date upon request by either party.

_____
Chairman of the Board
New Partner Ministry

_____
Charles T. Bennett
President
Partners International

_____
Name
Title
Partner

_____
Alexandre C. Araujo
Director
International Operations
Partners International

Date: _____

Date: _____

Addenda:
Principles and Policies for Cooperative Work

Partners International exists to participate with Christian ministries throughout the world to fulfill the Great Commission. This is accomplished through complementary partnership—the mutual sharing of vision, capabilities, and material resources. PI seeks to establish cooperative relationships with organizations whose basic values and goals agree with its own.

Principles of Partnership

1. That any God-honoring service should be carried out in a spirit of mutual respect, trust, and submission to the Lord (Gal. 5:13).

2. That mutual accountability is an integral aspect of Christian stewardship (1 Cor. 4:2; Rom. 14:12).

Policies for Cooperative Work

Partnership in missions is the temporary affiliation of independent ministries by which one serves to fill out or complete the other within the framework of a common goal, and in support of this position to:

1. Subscribe to the foundational doctrines of Scripture.

2. Agree that each party will be overseen by a duly constituted governing body or board made up largely of local responsible individuals.

3. Perceive each to be independent of the other, and agree that neither should interfere in the administration of the other.

4. Agree to work within the framework of a working agreement which is drawn up through a collaborative process.

Partners International

In cooperation with the New Partner, PI is committed to:

1. Pursue with integrity a policy of complementary assistance to the partner ministry and its members in accordance with a written mutually acceptable working agreement.

2. Publish its audited financial report annually and send a copy to the partner ministry upon request.

3. Honor the donor's intent by transferring all funds as designated with the understanding that certain overhead costs are deducted.

4. Give a full explanation of its relationship with the New Partner in any publicity, so as not to confuse the public or discredit or violate the indigenous nature of the partner ministry.

5. Foster a continuing prayer burden for the partner ministry and a financial interest in it by making available information about the ministry; assist in the development of a donor base; arrange deputation programs if and when necessary.

6. Contribute to the self-developing capabilities of the partner ministry.

Partner Ministry

In cooperation with PI, the New Partner is committed to:

1. Maintain the partnership according to the mutually acceptable working agreement.

2. Permit PI to represent and publicize its projects and programs, providing there is no likelihood of adverse effect on the partner ministry.

3. Keep PI fully informed of the general situation of its ministry and the progress of the specific assistance program and provide an audited financial report annually to PI.

4. Inform PI when partner ministry personnel travel in countries where PI has an associated council and ensure that ministry personnel abide by the established deputation program when invited by PI to travel abroad to promote ministry projects.

5. Maintain the indigenous nature of the ministry and strengthen its self-developing capabilities.

6. Provide PI with periodic reports on all projects. Avoid obligation to PI for projects not duly approved for funding.

7. Provide the following for the Sponsor-A-National Program:

• Worker personal data on a standard form with a colored photograph and negative and a personal testimony.

• Two (2) prayer letters per year from each worker (specifically in May and September).

• An annual report from the ministry leader in January.

(Note: The number of workers in this program may or may not affect the amount of the monthly allocation.)

Statement of Faith

We believe:

• That both Old and New Testaments constitute the divinely inspired Word of God, inerrant in the originals.

• In one God existing eternally in three persons, Father, Son, and Holy Spirit.

• That the Lord Jesus Christ, the Son of God, became Man without ceasing to be God, in order that He might reveal God and redeem sinful men.

• That the Holy Spirit came forth from the Father and the Son to convict the world of sin, of righteousness, and of judgment; and to regenerate, sanctify, comfort, and seal those who believe in Jesus Christ; and to empower them to use spiritual gifts for the carrying out of the work of the Lord Jesus Christ.

• That man is totally depraved in that of himself he is utterly unable to remedy his lost condition.

• That salvation of man's eternal being is the gift of God brought to man by grace and received by personal faith in the Lord Jesus Christ, whose atoning blood was shed on the cross for the forgiveness of sin.

• In the baptism by water of believers, symbolizing the believer's union in the death and resurrection of Jesus Christ.

• In the observance of the Lord's Supper, commemorating the sacrifice of our Savior for all mankind.

• That the life of the believer is to be separate from worldliness by consistent conduct before God and man, and is to be in the world as lifegiving light.

• In the personal, visible, bodily, and imminent return of the Lord Jesus Christ, and that His second advent is essential to the fulfillment of God's plan for this age.

APPENDIX 3

Missions Standards in India: An Appeal to All Overseas Partners

We are grateful to God for your interest in India. Some of you are supporting some work somewhere in India. Until now there was no referral point in India to provide you objective appraisal of the performance standards of the Indian work you are supporting. You had to depend on your own remote sensing or on some subjective perception or information.

Now you can and therefore you must obtain official, objective, and comprehensive appraisal of the work you support. Missions Standards Cell provides you that. Write immediately to MSC. Several works (or workers) of God in India are seriously damaged by indiscreet funding from overseas, about which the leaders in India are greatly concerned.

You may be a person or mission interested in supporting a new work/workers in India. If so, you must first ascertain the credibility of the persons, the viability of their structure, and the suitability of duplicity of the program in the context. Missions Standards Cell provides this information. Contact MSC immediately before you take the next step.

Missions Standards Cell is a partly autonomous body under India Missions Association, governed and run by a 15-member Advisory Committee of eminent and committed Christian professionals and highly experienced mission leaders. Missions Standards Cell is the only body in India which can provide the most objective and comprehensive reference. Write today for the brochure and forms of MSC.

Missions Standards Cell
Post Box 2529
Madras-600 030
INDIA
Phone: (044) 612870
Cable: INMISSIONS

APPENDIX 4

Consultation Participants

World Evangelical Fellowship
Missions Commission Consultation
"Towards Interdependent Partnership"
Manila, June 1992

Participant List

Howard Ahmanson, Fieldstead and Co., California, USA

Devine Amattey, Ghana Evangelical Missions Association, Ghana

Walo Ani, Papua New Guinea Missionary Association, Papua New Guinea

Kong Yow Aow, Singapore Center for Evangelism and Missions, Singapore

Alex Araujo, Partners International, California, USA

John Abu Bakker, India

Herbert Beerens, Prairie Graduate School, Canada

Federico Bertuzzi, Misiones Mundiales, Argentina

Nell Binayao, Translators Association of the Philippines, Philippines

Barbara Burns, Brazil

Phillip Butler, Interdev, Washington, USA

Herbert Cann, Overseas Council for Theo. Ed. and Mission, UK

Pablo Carrillo Luna, PM International, Spain

Met Castillo, Missions Commission/Evangelical Fellowship of Asia, Philippines

David Dong-Jin Cho, Asia Missions Association, Korea

Steve Cochrane, YWAM, India

Ruben Conner, Black Evangelistic Enterprise, Texas, USA

David Cummings, Wycliffe Bible Translators, Australia

Stanley Davies, EMA, UK

Dan Davis, Hope Chapel/Antioch Network, Texas, USA

Warner Dickson, Interdev, Washington, USA

Bruce Dipple, SIM Australia, Australia

Arsenio Dominguez, Philippine Missionary Institute, Philippines

Robert C. Douglas, Zwemer Institute of Muslim Studies, California, USA

Mark K. Dyer, International Teams, Illinois, USA

Roger Dyer, Australia

Bertil Ekstrom, Brazilian Association of Cross-Cultural Missions, Brazil

James Engel, Center for Organizational Excellence/Eastern College, Pennsylvania, USA

Bayo Famonure, Evangelism and Missions Commission/ AEAM, Nigeria

Robert Ferris, Columbia Bible College and Seminary, South Carolina, USA

Gene Flanery, World Indigenous Missions, Philippines

Maher Fouad, AWEMA, Egypt

Takashi Fukuda, Wycliffe Bible Translators, Japan

Rodolfo Girón, COMIBAM, Guatemala

Dave Hane, Church of the Nazarene, Asia Pacific Regional Office, Philippines

Victor Hashweh, Arab World Evangelical Ministers Association, UK

Albrecht Hauser, Evangelical Lutheran Church of Wuerttemberg, Germany

Keith Hinton, Bible College Victoria/Center of World Mission, Australia

Daniel Ho Kang Chan, National Evangelical Christian Fellowship, Malaysia

Steve Hoke, Church Resource Ministries, California, USA

Tom Houston, Lausanne Committee for World Evangelization, UK

Tom Yong-Hyun Hwang, Korean Center for World Missions, Korea

M. Patrick Joshua, Friends Missionary Prayer Band, India

Hans Keijzer, Evangelical Missionary Alliance, Netherlands

Larry Keyes, OC International, Colorado, USA

Tui Komia, PNGNCEC, Papua New Guinea

Dietrich Kuhl, WEC International, UK

Maikudi Kure, Evangelical Missionary Society, Nigeria

J. Paul Landrey, Latin America Mission, Florida, USA

Vic Lazarus, Missions Commission/Evangelical Fellowship of South Africa, South Africa

David Tai-Woong Lee, Global Ministry Training Center, Korea

Jonathan Lewis, WEF Missions Commission, Florida, USA

Hoe Peng Loh, WEF Missions Commission, Singapore

Alvin Low, AD 2000 and Beyond Movement, Colorado, USA

Michael Maeliau, Evangelical Fellowship of S.P., Solomon Islands

Patrick Marman, Discipleship Training Center, Singapore

Robert Martin, First Fruit Inc., California, USA

Peter Maru, Africa Inland Church Missionary Board, Kenya

Brian Massey, Asia Pacific Christian Mission, Australia

Thomas H. McAlpine, World Vision, California, USA

Thomas H. McCallie III, The Maclellan Foundation, Tennessee, USA

Paul McKaughan, Evangelical Fellowship of Mission Agencies, Washington DC, USA

Lois McKinney, Trinity Evangelical Divinity School, Illinois, USA

Carl McMindes, Gospel Missionary Union, Missouri, USA

Ato Worabo Mennu, Kale Hiwot Church, Ethiopia

Len Norton, SEND International, Philippines

Joshua Ogawa, Japan Evangelical Association, Japan

Minoru Okuyama, Asia Missions Association, Japan

John Orme, Interdenominational Foreign Mission Association, Illinois, USA

Greg H. Parsons, US Center for World Mission, California, USA

Larry Pate, OC International, California, USA

David Pickard, OMF International, Singapore

Jonathan F. Santos, Antioch Mission/AMT3, Brazil

Benjamin Saoshiro, Department of World Missions/ Immanuel General Mission, Japan

Donald Schmierer, Fieldstead and Co., California, USA

Gerry Seale, EAC/PAWI, Barbados

Patrick Sookhdeo, SFI/In-Contact Ministries, UK

Theodore Srinivasagam, Indian Evangelical Mission, India

Ebenezer Sunder Raj, India Missions Association, India

Sam Kang Sung, Korea World Missions Association, Korea

Bertin Svensson, Swedish Missionary Council, Sweden

Toshio Takshashi, Evangelical Free Church of Japan, Japan

Ray Tallman, Arab World Ministries, Illinois, USA

John D. Tanner, Missions Commission/Evangelical Alliance, Australia

Paul Taylor, Mission to the World, Georgia, USA

William D. Taylor, WEF Missions Commission, Texas, USA

James A. Tebbe, Interserve, Cyprus

Kenneth A. Thompson, LOGOI International, Florida, USA

Bill Waldrop, ACMC, Illinois, USA

Ronald A. Wiebe, SIM, North Carolina, USA

Theodore Williams, World Evangelical Fellowship, India

Raymond Windsor, WEF Missions Commission, New Zealand

Ralph D. Winter, William Carey International University, California, USA

APPENDIX 5
Bibliography

1. *Partnership: Accelerating Evangelism in the '90s*, by Phill Butler with Clyde Cowan. An Interdev publication produced in partnership with Advancing Churches in Missions Commitment (ACMC) and the Missions Commission of World Evangelical Fellowship. An excellent 32-page booklet with the basics on partnership through action steps for missions, churches, and donors, resources, and some of the "how to." Order for US$1.50 from WEF, P.O. Box WEF, Wheaton, IL 60189, USA.

2. *Partners in the Gospel: The Strategic Role of Partnership in World Evangelization*, edited by James H. Kraakevik and Dotsey Welliver, published by the Billy Graham Center, Wheaton College, Wheaton, IL 60187, USA. 203 pages, US$6.95. This book is an excellent resource to learn partnership concepts and how others have advanced evangelism through successful partnerships.

3. *Partnership Diagnostic Kit.* Interdev has developed a diagnostic tool to evaluate partnerships. The goal is to strengthen and make the partnership more effective in reaching the unreached for Christ. If you would like a copy, please contact Interdev, P.O. Box 30945, Seattle WA 98103, USA; or P.O. Box 47, Ashford, Middlesex TW15 2LX, England.

4. *Partnership for Profit: Structuring and Managing Strategic Alliances*, by Professor Jordan D. Lewis, Wharton School of Business. Phill Butler recommends this significant work on the subject from the secular perspective, which clearly understands the need for and power of these national and international alliances.

5. *Partnering in Ministry: The Direction of World Evangelism*, by Luis Bush and Lorry Lutz, Downers Grove, IL, USA, Inter-Varsity Press, 1990. A more popular development of the theme with specific guidelines and a sample working agreement from Partners International.

Index